CONCORDIA UNIVERSITY

ML3100.T5   C001
MUSIC IN CHRISTIAN EDUCATION NASHV

3 4211 000064171

S0-BHY-437

MUSIC

IN

CHRISTIAN EDUCATION

THE COOPERATIVE SERIES
Leadership·Training Textbooks

Many thousands of lay workers in Protestant churches attend interdenominational leadership education schools each year. It is essential that the courses offered and the text materials used be acceptable to the many varieties of Protestant groups found in our American communities.

The Cooperative Series of leadership education textbooks are produced to meet that need. They are planned by the Division of Christian Education of the National Council of the Churches of Christ in the U.S.A., representing thirty-nine Protestant denominations. The Cooperative Publication Association, an interdenominational group of denominational editors and publishers selects the writers and provides editorial supervision to insure sound educational values, practical usefulness and interdenominational approval and acceptance.

MUSIC IN CHRISTIAN EDUCATION

Through Study and Practice

EDITH LOVELL THOMAS

PUBLISHED FOR

The Cooperative Publication Association

BY

ABINGDON-COKESBURY PRESS
New York   •   Nashville

MUSIC IN CHRISTIAN EDUCATION

Copyright MCMLIII by Pierce & Washabaugh

All rights in this book are reserved.
No part of the book may be used or reproduced in any
manner whatsoever without written permission of the
publishers except brief quotations embodied in critical
articles or reviews. For information address Abingdon-
Cokesbury Press, 810 Broadway, Nashville 2, Tennessee.

Library of Congress Catalog Card Number: 52-12169

The Bible: A New Translation by James Moffatt, copy-
righted 1922, 1935, 1950, by Harper & Brothers; *The
Bible: An American Translation* by Smith and Goodspeed, copyright 1935, by the University of Chicago.

SET UP, PRINTED, AND BOUND BY THE
PARTHENON PRESS, AT NASHVILLE,
TENNESSEE, UNITED STATES OF AMERICA

39630

PRELUDE

ONLY music that is audible is really music. The composer starts the musical process by putting signs on paper to be followed. Not until singers and players of instruments transform the signs into sounds does music come alive.

Because of this obvious fact the invitation to *sing* is written large across these pages. To *make* music is the primary purpose of assembling for this study that we may set others to singing with meaning and beauty.

> You ask me . . .
> What is the supreme happiness here below?
> It is listening to the song of a little girl
> As she goes down the road
> After having asked me the way.[1]

By practice we would learn what to sing. Through study and comment regarding the music and the words it accompanies we will seek to gain understanding of how, when, and where they can serve the needs of growing Christians.

Each session starts, ends, and is illustrated freely throughout with musical examples to make specific my discussion as the course unfolds. I have avoided expressing mere theories that I cannot match with music sung and played, or with records to which we listen. By such practice we test the values recommended as they are tried out in immediate singing experiments.

As musical messengers to the home, the school, and the community from the church, renewed through the power of Christian song, we dedicate our gifts to the glory of God and the re-creation of his children. A high commission we accept in humility—to learn how to inspire children, youth, and adults to sing for joy together.

[1] Wang-Wei (699-759).

CONTENTS

CONTENTS

CHAPTER I

REJOICING CHRISTIANS

Let the inspiration of Christ dwell in your midst with
all its wealth of wisdom; teach and train one another
with the music of psalms, with hymns, and songs of
the spiritual life; praise God with thankful hearts.[1]

Today and Yesterday

"FROM the days of primitive man, the arts have been the
means employed by human beings for direct communication with
the unseen." [2]

Through music Christians today, as always and everywhere, ac-
knowledge their dependence upon God for their very lives. Martin
Luther described how direct are the means of communication between God and his children, when he said, "Our dear Lord speaks
to us through his Holy Word, and we in return speak with him
through prayer and song of praise." And again, "It is my intention to
make German Psalms for the people—spiritual songs, that is, whereby
the word of God may be kept alive in them by singing."

The voice of song is never silent where Christianity lives. Listen
to the individual or the company singing to know what is cared
about most, "for a man's mouth utters what his heart is full of." [3]
The mood of joy, arising from the recognition of its Source, is as
old as man's discovery that he could make music, and it is as young
as today's gratitude, unfulfilled until sung.

What modes does the singing spirit infuse with life in our day?
Do they resemble the modes adopted by former Christian experience?
Pick up from here and there, from the present and past, fragments
of the unceasing song of faith, hope, and love, which characterize our
religion at its best. Listen! Over a kind of wireless connect with our
world-wide fellowship!

[1] Colossians 3:16 Moffatt (Paul writing to new Christians).
[2] Satis N. Coleman, *Your Child's Music* (The John Day Co.). Used by permission.
[3] Luke 6:45 Moffatt.

In China, Under Criticism

A meeting is being conducted by the culture department of the new "People's Government." Three members represent the Christian Church. As educational leaders they have succeeded in getting several obnoxious regulations changed. Before going into this conference they prayed earnestly for guidance. An official, whose daughter goes to a mission school, speaks against the Christian "superstition" of saying grace before meals. The president of a girls' college feels "the Holy Spirit boost" her to her feet. She meets the criticism by starting to sing a grace used by her students. In her eagerness she forgets her lack of musical gift for an instant, then calls to her aid the principal of a boys' school. Together they sing:

> Lord, before we eat
> We want to remember in thanksgiving
> All the farmers, who planted our food,
> All the others who prepared it,
> The sun and the rain from God,
> The Creator of all.[4]

The confession of faith is convincing. The culture department is won over by this witness to Christian education in the daily round, clothed in music. The commentator adds, "When these representatives speak they are listened to because of their wealth of experience and depth of insight, backed up with solid Christian character. I suspect this is the hope all over China." [5]

Can anyone estimate the power of *Hymns of Universal Praise* [6] to enable Chinese Christians to meet the tests put to them in days like these? Working with missionary friends the Chinese made this unique hymnal out of newly composed Oriental hymns and tunes, coupled with those from Western churches, which expressed their convictions. Chinese folk tunes, never before dedicated so extensively to sacred use, in this book have become a new medium through which modern Christian experiences are being shared. In one instance the ancient "Farmers' Song of the Hoe" has been elevated to the hymn level and set to words which confess dependence upon God for life itself:

---

[4] From a letter written in China by a Protestant missionary, 1950. Used by permission.
[5] *Ibid.*
[6] Hymnal published in Chinese by the Church of Christ in China.

Great are thy mercies, heavenly Father,
All our food and shelter come from thee;
Serving thee every day,
Humbly would I live.
I'm a tender blade of grass—
Breathe on me!

Bliss Wiant, musical editor of this collection, says of it, "There is no hymnal in all Christendom which serves such a diverse group of Christian worshippers. Practically every denomination in China uses this one hymnal." With what strength they can unite in worship, nourished by the spiritual food these hymns supply!

In "Times of Trouble and Persecution"

Not once but many times in John Wesley's *Journal* is found the record of virulent attacks upon his person and frightful attempts to stop him from preaching. Unflinchingly he took the advice he gave his converts, "Always look a mob in the face." Read about this amazing encounter which occurred October 20, 1743:

The mob of Walsal came, pouring in like a flood, and bore down all before them. The Darlaston mob made what defence they could; but they were weary, as well as outnumbered; so that in a short time, many being knocked down, the rest ran away, and left me in their hands.

To attempt speaking was vain, for the noise on every side was like the roaring of the sea. So they dragged me along till we came to the town, where, seeing the door of a large house open, I attempted to go in; but a man, catching me by the hair, pulled me back into the middle of the mob. They made no more stop till they had carried me through the main street, from one end of the town to the other. I continued speaking all the time to those within hearing, feeling no pain or weariness. At the west end of the town, seeing a door half open, I made toward it, and would have gone in; but a gentleman in the shop would not suffer me, saying they would pull the house down to the ground. However, I stood at the door and asked, "Are you willing to hear me speak?" Many cried out, "No, no! knock his brains out; down with him; kill him at once." Others said, "Nay, but we will hear him first." I began asking, "What evil have I done? Which of you all have I wronged in word or deed?" and continued speaking for above a quarter of an hour, till my voice suddenly failed. Then the floods began to lift up their voice again, many crying out, "Bring him away! Bring him away!"

In the meantime my strength and my voice returned, and I broke out aloud into prayer. And now the man who just before headed the mob, turned and said, "Sir, I will spend my life for you: follow me, and not one soul here shall touch a hair of your head." . . .

11

God brought me safe to Wednesbury; having lost only one flap of my waistcoat, and a little skin from one of my hands.

I never saw such a chain of providences before; so many convincing proofs that the hand of God is on every person and thing, overruling all as it seemeth him good.

Out of turmoil convictions were forged which shaped the Methodist movement that John and his brother Charles promoted, creating hymns to match emergency. One of the number holds these lines:

Ye servants of God, your Master proclaim,

· · · · · · · · ·

The floods they are roaring, but Jesus is here,

· · · · · · · · ·

Their fury shall never our steadfastness shock,

· · · · · · · · ·

And still he is nigh, his presence we have.[7]

Reinforced by this hymn throngs of common people faced the violent mob in England over two hundred years ago in outdoor meetings. The Wesley brothers, founders of the Methodist movement, were falsely accused of political intrigue. Above the clamor of opposition, they proclaimed in song their confidence in Christ. Vast crowds of people joined in singing, uncowed by hostility. Charles Wesley created this hymn for this specific purpose. Thousands of hymns he wrote to meet almost every conceivable situation. His brother John taught the multitudes to sing them from the heart, and the resulting revival of religion "changed the face of England" and swept over the world.

Gathered Together the People Began to Sing

It was in Norway. The Nazis had gained control of the land, and the stunned, bewildered people picked themselves up and tried to go on with their regular lives. They turned to the church for help, and their church did not fail them. Their pastors and bishops spoke out fearlessly against the wrong in the new regime. One Sunday there was to be a service in the cathedral and their beloved bishop was to speak. The people thronged to the church, but when they got there, they learned that their leader was in prison for his unyielding opposition to the Nazis.

Their church doors were locked. But the people gathered together in the

[7] From the hymn "Ye Servants of God, Your Master Proclaim," by Charles Wesley. See Robert Guy McCutchan, *Our Hymnody* (Abingdon-Cokesbury Press), for its story and the stanzas usually omitted.

square in front of the church, and without anyone suggesting it, they began to sing. "A Mighty Fortress Is Our God" rang through the streets.

Do you wonder that this hymn is called the "Battle Song of the Reformation"? It is more than that. It is a battle song against tyranny and wrong in any age, or in any place.[8]

"Religious Experience at White Heat"

Roland Hayes, the great Negro tenor, tells of the marvel of song arising out of slavery.

I was born just twenty-four years after the Emancipation Proclamation. The atmosphere of the slave days was still strong at my place of birth and the religious folk songs of my people were being born out of religious experience at white heat. . . .

Drawing on his reservoir of musical instinct, embracing Old and New Testaments with the tenacity of a plant, [the Aframerican] sank his roots deep down into its Truth, bringing both Old and New Testaments into close relationship with himself with utter naturalness and proper perspective. . . .

My people found in the grandeur of the Biblical word and poetry a fountain of illimitable solace. From out the horizon of their tragic lot rose a sublime illumination; an all-stimulating ray of hope for deliverance through the Star of Bethlehem. Its radiance fostered a faith in its promise that drew inspiration in endless play of imagination around the revelations of the Bible. This enduring Faith moved with complete confidence amid its allegories, symbols and parables. Word and music became one; the religious ecstasy as well as sheer intoxication with the sound of the Word itself flowing forth into exciting expansions of religious experience.[9]

A Family Canticle

While working on this book and writing down the memories of a family, it astonished, amazed, almost overwhelmed me to see how much love—genuine, real love—was stored up in one short lifetime: first, God's love for us his children, the leading, guiding, protecting love of a Father; and as every real love calls forth love in return, it couldn't be any different here. . . .

As we are singers, this story turned into a song, a canticle. . . . "Sing unto the Lord a new song." . . . *The Story of the Trapp Family Singers* wants to be a canticle of love and gratitude to the Heavenly Father in his Divine Providence.[10]

This chronicle as set down by the mother is a remarkable record of the influence of singing on a family at home, in camp, and in

[8] Catherine and Frank Herzel, *To Thee We Sing* (Muhlenberg Press), pp. 76, 77. Used by permission.

[9] Roland Hayes, *My Songs* (Little, Brown & Co.), pp. vii, 12, 13. Used by permission.

[10] Maria Augusta Trapp, *The Story of the Trapp Family Singers* (J. B. Lippincott Co.), pp. 7, 8. Used by permission.

concerts all over this country—carols, folk songs, chorales, and great church music.

"The Inspiration of Christ"

Seeds which grew into the Christian Church sprang from a three-fold sacrament. First, a humble act of service to daily physical need, washing the feet of his disciples by the Master-Servant. Then a supper of bread and wine, the fellowship of friends, and last, singing a joyful festival hymn by Jesus and eleven of his followers, their final act of dedication and march to the cross. While there is universal honor shown toward the second and slight attention is paid to the first, have we underestimated the significance of the sacrament of song?

What meaning had this for Jesus? Matthew and Mark report in terse words, "And when they had sung a hymn, they went out to the Mount of Olives." [11] The supper is linked to the hymn with an "and." Jesus had just explained to his friends the significance of the shared meal as the "new covenant" to be observed in remembrance of him. Immediately there followed the signing of this compact, so to speak, by the united voices of the men and their Leader singing the hymn of allegiance. Did not this hymn become the climax of the course taken with the greatest Teacher when he sang it with his class during the final moment of worship?

Was it not also a preparation for the ordeals which came in swift succession—the agony in the garden, the trial, and death? What act could bind these men more firmly together and to their Master in a sacred brotherhood? How could they more fervently declare their trust in the Father's new and living way, which they were called to promote? Although glimpsed dimly by the men, Jesus with clear vision must have been nerving them for their high destiny while renewing his own courage and faith.

"Train One Another with the Music of Psalms" [12]

What hymn was adequate to support these singers on this Holy Thursday? To what music was it sung? When was it learned? A host of questions arises. In moments of crisis that which is most ingrained in a person's character is apt to come to the surface. Forms of expression associated with one's religious training have tremendous driving power and are ready resources when need for them is urgent. A

[11] Matthew 26:30; Mark 14:26 R.S.V.
[12] Colossians 3:16 Moffatt.

reasonable assumption is that the hymn which came to Jesus' lips was the first great Hallelujah chorus that originated with his own people. Sung in celebration of Jewish feast days—Passover, Pentecost, and Tabernacles—it was taught to children early and as they matured was always interwoven with their most sacred memories. Since the last days of the life of Jesus fell in Passover week, what more natural choice could be made than the Passover hymn of joy?

However, singing a traditional hymn in observance of an old custom would hardly be sufficient reason for its selection at this crucial hour. The hymn must also be a true medium for the surging emotions that all but engulfed the little company. It had to be a declaration of confidence in a God who would not fail them as they were put to the supreme test. The final section of the Hallelujah hymn (Psalms 113-18) is the portion that may have been appropriated, some scholars think. Examine it to determine whether or not it might fulfill the demands of Jesus for this sacrament of song with his disciples. (See pp. 17, 19.)

To what music was the hymn sung?

Does anything remain of the rich musical service which for fifteen hundred years went up daily from tabernacle and temple to the throne of the God of Israel? . . . With the possible exception of scanty fragments, nothing remains of the songs so much loved by this devoted people in their early home. We may speculate upon the imagined beauty of that music. . . . We know that it often shook the hearts of those that heard it; but our knowledge of the comparative rudeness of all Oriental music, ancient and modern, teaches us that its effect was essentially that of simple unison successions of tones wedded to poetry of singular exaltation and vehemence, and associated with liturgical actions calculated to impress the beholder with an overpowering sense of awe. . . . This music foreshadowed the completer expression of Christian art of which it became the type. . . . The soul of music passed from Hebrew priests to apostles and Christian fathers, and so on to the saints and hierarchs, who laid the foundation of the sublime structure of the worship music of a later day.[13]

Whatever fragments survive from the music of Jesus' day, if any, have come to us by way of oral tradition because a precise system of writing down notes on a staff was not developed until many centuries later.

It is inferred from the structure of the Hebrew poetry, as well as unbroken usage from the beginning of the Christian era, that the psalms were chanted

[13] Edward Dickinson, *Music in the History of the Western Church* (Charles Scribner's Sons, 1927), pp. 33, 34, 35. Used by permission.

15

antiphonally or responsively. . . . The Oriental Christians sang the psalms responsively; this method was passed on to Milan in the fourth century, to Rome very soon afterward, and has been perpetuated in the liturgical churches of modern Christendom.[14]

When did Jesus and his comrades learn the Passover hymn? Doubtless they were taught it at home and in the synagogue school in boyhood as a part of their education in the Jewish faith. The hymn belonged to the

commemoration of Israel's exodus from Egypt as recorded in Exodus 12. It was a home-celebration par excellence. The ceremonies observed therein are intended to remind the Jewish people of the great event when God redeemed them from bondage and made them a free people dedicated to serve the eternal God only. All customs are therefore attuned to the aim of stirring in both old and young the spirit of liberty, of spiritual and physical freedom. The story and songs implant within one the conviction of the ultimate victory of individual freedom, of light succeeding darkness, and of ethical relationship superceding tyranny.[15]

How deep lie the roots of Christian song reaching back into the experience of Jesus, nourished by the best in his Hebrew training, quickened in his disciples by his insight and vivid use! Singing with the spirit and understanding was tended with care by apostles as they propagated the good news of Christ. The growth that has sprouted from these shoots has produced fruitage that has sustained succeeding generations to this very day. Upon us is laid the obligation to plant children by the stream of living hymns where there is depth of soil and favorable conditions for their growth in singing religion. The main purpose of this study and experiment is the culture of the spirit by means of musical impression and expression worthy of the sources which produced and nourished singing Christians. As we become sensitive to our trust, shall we not pray:

O Lord, who hast taught us that thou wilt require much of those to whom much has been given, grant that we who have received so goodly a heritage may strive to extend to others what we so richly enjoy; and, as we have entered into the labors of other men, so to labor that in their turn other men may enter into ours, to the fulfillment of thy holy will.[16]

[14] *Ibid.*, pp. 28, 29.
[15] A. Z. Idelsohn, *The Jewish Liturgy* (Henry Holt & Co., 1932) , p. 173. Used by permission.
[16] St. Augustine (adapted) .

We can claim the guidance of the same Spirit that was conferred upon the early church for we, like them, when "they were all together," are seeking the Way. Music is one of the surest means by which we experience our sense of oneness without which we have no true fellowship. Through singing in chorus we each and all have access to the same realm of delight. "Joy at its purest is the sign-manual of reality. In the moment of pleasure lies the certainty of Truth. It is the tasting of God in whom is ever perfect joy." [17] Let us rejoice then in our birthright of song and "teach and *train one another* with the music of psalms"!

PRACTICE SINGING TOGETHER

"Attend strictly to the sense of what you sing and see that your heart is not carried away with the sound, but offered to God continually." [18]

Joyful Prelude in Remembrance of Jesus: A Hymn

Sing "A Christian Greeting": "May Jesus Christ be Praised!"

Hallelujah: Passover Psalm

Read. (Punctuate with silence between verses. Ponder its meaning for Jesus and his disciples as it might be a sacrament of song on the eve of the crucifixion.)

O give thanks unto the Lord; for he is good: because his mercy endureth for ever. Let Israel now say, that his mercy endureth for ever.
(*Gratitude for changeless, compassionate Goodness.*)

I called upon the Lord in distress: the Lord answered me, and set me in a large place.
(*Divine release—response to cry for help.*)

The Lord is on my side: I will not fear: what can man do unto me?
(*Powerful Helper inspires courage for emergency.*)

It is better to trust in the Lord than to put confidence in man.
(*Faith in Unseen born of experience.*)

The Lord is my strength and song, and is become my salvation. The voice of rejoicing and salvation is in the tabernacles of the righteous; the right hand of the Lord doeth valiantly.
(*Fortitude, joy, confidence, victory.*)

[17] A. D. Martin, *A Plain Man's Life of Christ.* Copyright 1947 by The Macmillan Co. and used with their permission.
[18] John Wesley.

LAUDES DOMINI

Joseph Barnby

1. When morning gilds the skies,
   My heart, awaking, cries,
       May Jesus Christ be praised!
   When evening shadows fall,
   This rings my curfew call,
       May Jesus Christ be praised!

2. When mirth for music longs,
   This is my song of songs:
       May Jesus Christ be praised!
   God's holy house of pray'r
   Hath none that can compare
       With: Jesus Christ be praised!

3. Ye nations of mankind,
   In this your concord find:
       May Jesus Christ be praised!
   Let all the earth around
   Ring joyous with the sound:
       May Jesus Christ be praised! Amen.[19]

[19] Translated by Robert Bridges and reproduced from the *Yattendon Hymnal* by permission of the Clarendon Press, Oxford.

I shall not die, but live, and declare the works of the Lord. The Lord hath chastened me sore: but he hath not given me over unto death.

(*Hope not crushed despite darkest circumstances.*)

The Stone which the builders refused is become the head stone of the corner. This is the Lord's doing; it is marvellous in our eyes.

(*Wonder at God's way of working.*)

This is the day which the Lord hath made; we will rejoice and be glad in it.

(*Joyful acceptance of God's appointment.*)

Blessed be he that cometh in the name of the Lord: we have blessed you out of the house of the Lord.

(*High privilege of receiving a sacred messenger.*)

God is the Lord, which hath shewed us light: bind the sacrifice with cords, even unto the horns of the altar.

(*Illumination: making an offering.*)

Thou art my God, and I will praise thee: thou art my God, I will exalt thee. O give thanks unto the Lord; for he is good: for his mercy endureth for ever.

(*Exulting in a close relationship with the Eternal.*) [20]

Song of Gratitude for Our Hebrew Heritage

Sing "The Feast of Lights."

Tune: "Mooz Zur" ("Rock of Ages"), Old Synagogue Melody.

Sung at the Feast of Lights or Dedication, Chanukah, the celebration of the relighting of the lamps on the altar of the temple in Jerusalem. Historic background: Roman conquerors had used the temple for pagan worship until it was restored by Judas Maccabaeus to Jewish worship for which it was built.

Throughout this study and singing session we have been counting up our dividends as members of the fellowship of Christians. Are these among your receipts?

1. The lifting quality of poetry and music transmitted to us through the Hebrew-Christian tradition.

2. The vitality of Christian song in present daily experience "in the mind and on the lips."

3. Understanding something of what must have happened when Jesus and his friends sang a hymn together.

4. The contribution of the Psalms to our vocabulary of worship.

5. The unfailing joy of singing together.

---

[20] Parts of Psalm 118 K.J.V.

THE FEAST OF LIGHTS

From the German
Adapted by M. Jastrow and G. Gottheil

"Mooz Zur"
Old Synagogue Melody

1. Rock of A - ges, let our song Praise thy sav - ing pow - er;
2. Kind - ling new the ho - ly lamps, Priests ap - proved in suf - fer - ing,
3. Chil - dren of the Mar - tyr - race, Wheth - er free or fet - tered,

Thou, a - midst the rag - ing foes, Wast our shelter-ing tow - er.
Pur - i - fied the na - tion's shrine, Brought to God their of - fer - ing.
Wake the ech - oes of the songs Where ye may be scat - tered.

Fu - rious, they as - sailed us, But thine arm a - vail - ed us,
And his courts sur - round - ing Hear, in joy a - bound - ing,
Yours the mes - sage cheer - ing That the time is near - ing

And thy word Broke their sword When our own strength fail-ed us.
Hap - py throngs, Sing - ing songs With a might - y sound - ing.
Which will see All men free, Ty - rants dis - ap - pear - ing.

Used by permission of the Central Conference of American Rabbis.

CHAPTER II

FULFILLING THE MINISTRY OF SONG

... music is a house not made with hands,
Built by love's Father, where a little space
The soul may dwell; a royal palace fit
To meet the majesty of its demands;
The place where man's two lives unite;
the place
To hold communion with the infinite.[1]

What Is the Ministry of Song?

VIEW as in a candid camera shot the present ministry of music in the local church to which you belong. From this starting point study how to enlarge, alter, and quicken its vitality as you move forward in this course.

Toward what and whom are its services directed? How would you describe its features? Does it:

Call forth from every person it touches a singing spirit of joy, gratitude, and devotion to the Highest?

Stimulate the habit of singing together in the worship of the Unseen, with conviction and power?

Ground the people in hymns and tunes which inspire communion with God?

Familiarize singer and listener with larger choral and instrumental church music dedicated to religion—anthem, cantata, oratorio, and organ works written for the love of God?

Cultivate voices to express with spirit the outreaching of mind and heart in church school, choir, and congregation?

Prepare singers, through systematic training in church school and choir, to render offerings that have quality?

Relate to life the meanings of church ritual, sacrament, and ceremony, so that they fortify souls in time of suffering?

[1] Robert Haven Schauffler, "Music." By permission of the author.

Utilize the enjoyment and beauty of Christian song in every church organization to uplift, heal, and extend its service to those outside —the ill, the elderly, those in prison?

Now Is the Time

The church today, as custodian and representative of Christianity in a perilous period, must be true to her best tradition. Second-class and shabby song standards will not do. The memory of spiritual fathers must be kept alive to put iron into the blood. Witness to the truth newly discovered must steadily be breathed out in convincing music. We, in our day, have much more to sing about than even our courageous ancestors, who inscribed this summons on the walls of ancient Roman Catacombs to followers of Christ forced to meet in secrecy: "Gather together, O Christians, in these caverns, to read the holy books, to sing hymns, to pray. . . . There is light in this darkness. There is music in these tombs." [2]

Ministers of Song

A common belief is that the organist, who may also direct the choir, with more or less suggestion from the pastor, carries full responsibility for the musical program of both church and school. Only when this person is organist and/or director with due training should he be called the "Minister of Music." Sometimes the title is assumed without warrant, discrediting the office. So named, and in the light of present-day responsibilities, the office carries with it a larger scope than was previously visioned. Its holder should be capable of using sacred music to develop Christians who grow from infancy to maturity.

Whether or not a Minister of Music is employed, some one person usually has charge of the music. Whoever the individual may be, the larger outlook which the church is now adopting makes it plain that no one person can perform the task alone. He will enlist representatives from all the church organizations to help plan and forward the activities for each age level. Each person, then, who leads singing, accompanies, or conducts worship with any group is according to his ability a minister of song. Every leader requires guidance in order that he may contribute to the whole process. The musical head is to direct and co-ordinate their several efforts.

[2] W. H. Withrow, *The Catacombs of Rome* (Hodder & Stoughton, Ltd., London, 1895) , p. 148. Used by permission.

Pastor and music head, director of Christian education and church school supervisors in close relationship confer, recruit leaders, inspire associates, conduct services, and check and balance the results of the impact of music on the ones who are creating it. Responsibilities are divided so that each knows his own province. Director and minister superintend their helpers and make plain how the parts to be performed are related to the entire ministry.

The pastor looks upon the complete range of living from birth to death as the province of the church's care of *all* its people through preaching, worship, education, and recreation. Like the music director, he assigns many details and duties to others, but both keep a live contact with the church school. They regard it not as a separate unit, but as one integral aspect of the total ministry of the church. To change the figure, they tend it with great concern, for it is the seed plot from which the ultimate harvest of their labors is to be reaped.

One of the chief functions of the "Minister of the Word," as he is sometimes known, is to make the knowledge and application of hymns the bread of life to his parishioners. To help them appropriate this he serves it in an inviting way. One method is to print on the Sunday order of worship the words of a fine hymn week by week for a month. Families are encouraged to sing it at home. It is chosen with thought of children from primary years and on, and the minister, director, or other competent instructor teaches it in the church school departments, illuminated by story, picture, and comment. This custom is followed with a different hymn for each successive month for a year. By interpretation and repetition in church, school, and home during the month a series of hymns supplies a continual feast of song.

What are the hymns that hold something of common interest for young and older alike which strengthen their purpose to live like Christians? Consider what elements supply those required inner resources with which to meet each day with courage and adequacy. Look at this half dozen to see how they rate as hymn-of-the-month numbers to be learned and sung in church and home by older primary, junior, youth, and adult ages:

Praying and Purposing: "Lord, I want to be a Christian."
Seeing the Glory of God: "The heavens declare thy glory."
Expressing Joy and Wonder: "All creatures of our God and King."
Loving Our Neighbors: "In Christ there is no East or West," or "Re-

member all the people," or "Far round the world thy children sing their song."

Growing Kinship with Jesus: "We would see Jesus, lo! his star is shining."

Practicing Christian Conduct: "Be strong! We are not here to play, to dream, to drift."

Both minister and director are teachers who instruct the people in using the hymnal along with the Bible as their daily fare for living. They take every possible occasion to interpret how hymns sustain the spirit and build the sinews of character.

This was found on one church order of service:

> Hymn of the Month: During the fall and winter season we are hoping to add several hymns to our church's regular singing repertory. A hymn, relatively new to our congregation, will be selected each month, taught to the choirs, used in the church school classes, and in church services. Your active participation in this project will aid our worship.
>
> The hymn for October ("Come, my soul, thou must be waking," sung to the tune "Haydn," by Joseph Haydn) has been studied by the choir, used the past two Sundays in the services by the organist and Chancel Choir. Today and next Sunday it will be sung by the congregation. "The hymn is the people's expression of Christianity." Join expressively in the singing.[3]

When the music director knows children well and is skillful in drawing out their best, it is desirable that he lead church school singing as well as conduct student choirs. If he is unable to do this because of lack of personal fitness or press of other duties, a suitable associate should be found to fill the bill, perhaps a parent, superintendent, or teacher. The associate supplements and assists the director, discusses with the department heads about the music employed to relate it to other phases of the curriculum, study of hymns, group worship, and celebrations. Together these leaders try to correlate all means used to interest children and youth, enlarge their outlook, and enable them to sing well. They co-operate with teachers and parents (upon whom the main responsibility finally rests) to find ways of carrying over into life the values sought in school experiences.

The changing attitude of thoughtful leaders regarding the relative

[3] Highland Park Methodist Church, Dallas, Texas, "Choirs' Dedication and Preaching Service," October 22, 1950. Dr. Federal Lee Whittlesey, Minister of Music; Rev. Marshall T. Steel, Minister.

24

influence of church school music in its shaping of life is testified to by a Minister of Music in this letter recently received:

I teach classes in church music in . . . college and I do a good bit of teaching in summer courses and in workshops and seminars. For many years I was only partially interested in music in the church school, devoting most of my efforts to choirs, especially children's choirs. At last I have come to the conclusion that the church school plays a far more important part in the musical life of people than any other single part of church life and I am trying to reconstruct the program at my church.[4]

Reconstruction will involve the sorting out of what has come from the past, music that maintains the finest composers' thoughts devoted to religious ends; words and ideas that are simple, strong, and sufficient to awake in modern youth insights, new creations, conveying true ideals of growing Christians, and tunes and verse of the group's own making for voicing their convictions and dreams.

Provision in the year's round is made for each of these factors to educate young life in the things of the spirit which seek musical outlet. No church has a ministry worthy of the name that is not working earnestly, according to a purposeful design, to expose its children to values found in these basic materials. "Someone choose a number," or "What shall we sing today?" Casual bids thus thrown out to a group at the beginning of "opening exercises" or a so-called "worship service" are no substitute for understanding what is needed and furnishing substance fitted to meet the need.

Choir training is one of the dependable means of education which is utilized as early as is practicable, certainly at the junior stage. As a company of singers, prepared and imbued with the purpose to serve, boys and girls are able to minister through music in unique fashion. Though an individual's powers may be slight, in a group spiritual multiplication makes a force that transforms both singers and listeners in a miraculous way.

Take, then, as measures of the worth of your song ministry in its present state the personnel of its ministers, the number and quality of their associates, the scope of activities engaged in, and the impact being made on the lives of the persons it touches. What changes appear urgent? Face these problems.

[4] Mrs. T. J. Ingram, Jr., Minister of Music, Memorial Methodist Church, Lynchburg, Virginia.

On Whom Is the Ministry Focused?

The most active workers in the church are sometimes bothered about the lack of appreciation they receive and about how they stand in relative importance. The disciples argued over this issue, questioning Jesus, " 'Who is really greatest in the Kingdom of Heaven?' He called a child to him and had him stand among them, and he said, 'I tell you, unless you change and become like children, you will never get into the Kingdom of Heaven at all.' " [5]

When the spotlight is turned on the child, as he is allowed to "stand among" us, he becomes the center of our ministry and also the way to the finding of our own souls. The adult-child perspective insisted upon by Jesus is still a binding claim on every minister, director, leader of music, and teacher. Who among us must not change to achieve this controlling attitude of heart and mind? What study and spirit of humility it requires to practice it! Our ability to cope with adults depends upon our understanding of how they came to be the way they are and our entering into a child's thought, feeling, and acting as he matures. The church learns from and teaches its children in the school. The children learn from and teach their elders in the church.

However much religious training children receive at home, transmuting daily living into Christian character, every child requires worship and wider companionship which only his spiritual home, the church, can provide. How essential the ministry of this sort is to childhood, youth, and adulthood is gauged not so much by the budget, equipment, or size of staff but by less tangible factors.

The highest office the church can fulfill is to lead all its family in true worship. The smallest, most limited group can afford its people this privilege when minister, director, leader, choir, and congregation will unite in this supreme act. Each and all participate with heart and mind to make it genuine.

On minister and director devolve the selection and arrangement of the service elements. Individual parts are determined by the way each functions best and by the response expected from congregation and choir. The active, audible, congregational and choir portions, hymn, reading, prayer, offering, solo and anthem, are set in not because of convention but to evoke the co-operation upon which real worship depends. The rhythm and balance of parts taken

[5] Matthew 18:1-3 Goodspeed.

by leader and group are watched to keep the alternation of initiation and response fairly divided.

The choir performs the double purpose of helping the congregation to sing fervently, not substituting for the people's voices, and to lift the sight to new levels by bringing the listeners divine messages. Holding such ideals they prepare themselves for the sacrament of song, as ministering spirits, and assist also in silence. So a soloist is heard when a single voice can convey the thought better, and a younger or an older choir, or both, bear the "word of the Lord" to his waiting people, whichever can do it more clearly.

The organist's attitude toward the instrument he plays governs how well it fulfills its function. In what respects is it a tool? Is it for the training of young people, desirous of learning to play, for stimulating choir and congregation to worthy worship, for leading listeners to discover what noble church organ music can reveal of the glory of God? If the one who plays is indeed a minister, he will not think the organ belongs to him for his sole use, overpower those who try to sing to its accompaniment, or render sacred compositions to display his own ability.

In Protestant worship very much is required of the congregation by way of hearty singing of hymns, general responsive reading, and attentive silence in which to receive the ministry of pastor, organist, and choir. Being a witness to what is taking place is not enough, for Protestants believe that all the people, as well as the whole person, should engage in the worship ceremony. No priest or musician can be a substitute for the individual or company. How lifeless or ineffectual the process is when this principle is disobeyed! The cause of partial participation is sometimes found in the form or content offered, the way the service is conducted, or the lack of reality back of them. Sometimes the fault lies in the congregation when it fails to understand its own responsibility. Often both leaders and assembly need to reckon how their obligations, mutually binding, are being met.

One becomes a worshiper, as he becomes anything else, by learning the art of worship through instruction and practice. Beginning with the pastor and director every person who helps in the church's ministry is a teacher in word and example of the meaning and way of worship. Whether this teaching helps or hurts, it is a constant influence shaping the conceptions and attitudes of children, youth, and adults in regard to the place of worship in life.

The pastor does not have to be a musician to be a stimulator of those who take charge of choir and school music. Their efforts thrive or languish as he encourages, supports, and inspires the workers. To him the children and youth look for understanding and friendliness. With their welfare uppermost he secures the best obtainable leadership and maintains its standards. He visits their homes, school, and choir rehearsal. When they are in church service he tells them a story. When their choir appears, he makes their music an integral part of the entire act of worship, not merely a ruse to secure a larger attendance.

Instruction in worship is basic in the church school curriculum, and its study is put into practice as the children learn through experience its relation to living. Through this means there is training for church services, how to receive help from them and how to give to them what has been learned for the common good in song, group reading, or other form of expression in keeping with the occasion. These contributions are made by a department, class, or representative group, such as a singing or a speaking choir. The year's schedule is enlivened with as many dates for joint services as the church and school can make of mutual profit to younger and older folk alike. Their birthright as Christians will be entered into as they come to know the church's choicest music, well done by voices and instruments.

As the Choir Takes Its Task

In initial and regular contacts with each choir unit the director has the chance to make clear to the choristers their relationship to the church's ministry. Every member, however young or old, is both a recipient of and a contributor to its ministries in his capacity as a singer, player, and co-operator. Are your young people of musical promise being led into training for this ministry as a vocation?

The very title "Minister of Music," the seating of the choir within the chancel, the emphasis on participation in worship rather than putting on a show, all accent the co-operative nature of public devotions. More and more we are learning that music, as well as preaching, is a definite ministry in which leader, choir, and congregation are active agents.

To make this actual the director at first and frequently talks over with the choir his outlook on the work, its aim, quality, and demands. The choristers add ideas and raise questions about how they can measure up to the church's claim upon them. How to perform the right kind of messenger service for God and his people is their

39630

constant concern. Their spirit of dedication sometimes finds utterance in a choral prayer for fitness as in "Grace Before Singing":

> God of all lovely sounds, grant us a share
> In thy great harmonies of earth and air.
> Make us thy choristers, that we may be
> Worthy to offer music unto thee. Amen.[6]

The congregation creates the warmth of climate in which choirs can grow and bear fruit. Adults can and should surrender their sovereignty over the major part of the minister's time and attention. They can develop a church family atmosphere where all ages receive due share and each finds a place and fills it, holding respect for every other person.

Public recognition of the joint responsibility of congregation and choir is given when a service is devoted to emphasizing the meaning of this co-operative ministry. One church dignifies the choir office by dedicating the singers early in the fall. The members of all the choirs, called by name, come to the altar, take their vows of choir membership, and consecrate themselves in a ritual concluding with the congregation offering a prayer of consecration on this wise:

The Dedication of the Chancel Choir

Minister: You who with true stewardship of time and sacrifice, and who out of a deep love for the art of sacred music have committed yourselves to the religious discipline of its mastery, do you promise that by the help of God you will faithfully endeavor to meet the obligations of a choir member of this church?

Choir Members: In order to kindle the flame of devotion, that the people of God who assemble here may worship the Father in spirit and truth, and in order to bear up the melody of hymn and spiritual song in such wise that men may go forth from this house of God with high resolve to do his holy will, I do so promise, the Lord being my helper.

The Prayer of Consecration (choir kneeling)

Congregation: To the glory of God, author of all goodness and beauty, giver of skill of mind and voice and hand, we receive and dedicate these choirs. We promise to support them by our prayers, by the receptivity of our own hearts to the deeper meaning of the music which we hear and sing, by showing personal

---

[6] Anne Lloyd. Music by Clarence Dickinson (H. W. Gray Co.). Words reprinted by permission.

appreciation for the work which they do, by enlisting other voices for this important contribution to our church, and by joining with them in a fellowship of life and worship that shall be worthy in the sight of God.

Minister: Now unto Him that loved us and gave Himself for us, be all glory, praise and blessing forever and ever.[7]

Another church conducts a similar service in this form:

The Dedication of the Choirs

A Grace Before Singing: "God of All Lovely Sounds," Dickinson
The Presentation of the Choirs: Minister of Music
Choristers' Response: "Sing We All," Praetorius
Charge to the Choirs: The Minister
Litany of Dedication:

Leader: To a conduct of life worthy of those who stand before others in the public worship of God,
Choristers: We dedicate ourselves.
Leader: To help in the fostering of reverence in the House of God, and to the creating of an atmosphere of worship,
Choristers: We dedicate ourselves.
Leader: To lead the congregation in singing the praises of God, and giving the honor due unto his name,
Choristers: We dedicate ourselves.
Leader: To fill the hour of worship with song and praise and prayer, and to help as we can in the lifting of the burdens of life from all who enter here,
Choristers: We dedicate ourselves.
Leader: To lead others by song into the Kingdom of God,
Choristers: We dedicate ourselves.
Leader: To testify in glad and tuneful music our gratitude and love to Thee,
Choristers: We dedicate ourselves.
Choral Prayer: "Deepen My Music, O Lord," Conant.[8]

For a lifelike picture of how the ministry of song works out in the light of our study, draw a sketch of its features filling in details to match your own situation. Line in (1) a description of what makes your music a ministry to the people; (2) list the names and functions of those who are its ministers in all of its aspects; and (3) list

[7] Hamline Methodist Church, Washington, D.C., *Choir Dedication Service*, November 12, 1950. J. Edward Moyer, Minister of Music; Rev. J. A. Leatherman, Minister.
[8] Highland Park Methodist Church, *op. cit.*

changes necessary to reach every child, youth, and adult in the church's family, directly or indirectly.

APPLYING THE MINISTRY OF SONG

At Home: "Praise and Thanksgiving," Alsatian Round

Make a habit of singing together, at table, doing dishes, before the open fire, around the piano, for worship, etc.

Try this round to see how it sounds done in unison, two parts, and three parts. Call in neighbors for occasional sings.

PRAISE AND THANKSGIVING

Paraphrase of the German
Heartily

"Lobet und Praiset"
Alsatian Round

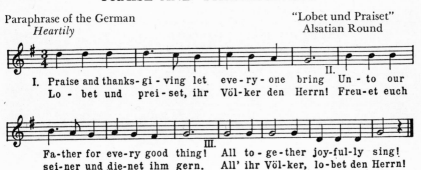

I. Praise and thanks-gi - ving let eve-ry - one bring Un - to our
Lo - bet und prei-set, ihr Völ-ker den Herrn! Freu-et euch

Fa-ther for eve-ry good thing! All to - ge-ther joy-ful-ly sing!
sei-ner und die-net ihm gern. All' ihr Völ-ker, lo-bet den Herrn!

Edith Lovell Thomas, *The Whole World Singing* (The Friendship Press, 1950), p. 103. Used by permission.

In Church School: "The Company of Jesus," J. S. Bach

To train our minds to choose the better part, to discipline our bodies to do our Father's work, to break down the barriers that separate those whom Jesus calls "friends," to live in the company of Jesus, to sing the music of one who deeply expresses his spirit, and to keep his purposes before us—let us learn to sing this chorale beautifully.

THE COMPANY OF JESUS

Edith Lovell Thomas
Eagerly

J. S. Bach, 1736

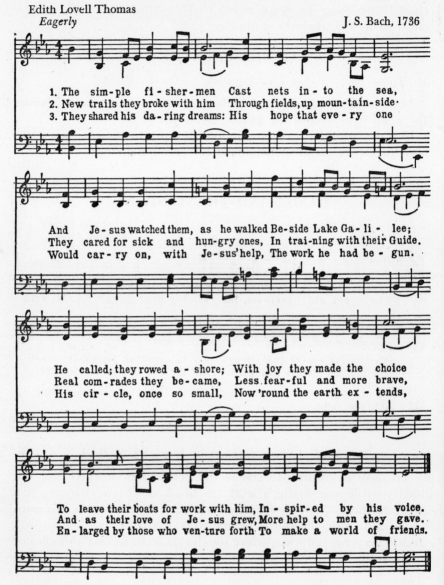

1. The sim-ple fi-sher-men Cast nets in-to the sea,
2. New trails they broke with him Through fields, up moun-tain-side·
3. They shared his da-ring dreams: His hope that eve-ry one

And Je-sus watched them, as he walked Be-side Lake Ga-li-lee;
They cared for sick and hun-gry ones, In trai-ning with their Guide.
Would car-ry on, with Je-sus' help, The work he had be-gun.

He called; they rowed a-shore; With joy they made the choice
Real com-rades they be-came, Less fear-ful and more brave,
His cir-cle, once so small, Now 'round the earth ex-tends,

To leave their boats for work with him, In-spir-ed by his voice.
And as their love of Je-sus grew, More help to men they gave.
En-larged by those who ven-ture forth To make a world of friends.

Edith Lovell Thomas, *The Whole World Singing*, p. 118. Copyright 1950 by Friendship Press, Inc. Used by permission.

At the Church: "The Church's One Foundation," S. S. Wesley

"Be grateful for receiving a kingdom that cannot be shaken, and thus let us offer to God acceptable worship, with reverence and awe." [9] Rejoice in the firm foundation on which the church rests, amid destructive influences which threaten to overthrow it. We sing a hymn of faith in the unity of Christians, to marching music, making it a reality wherever we go.

Experience this oneness by doing the first stanza in unison. Singing the second stanza in parts strengthens the impression of different elements blended to achieve a higher synthesis. A few high sopranos carrying the descant for a fifth part adds to the familiar music a refreshing quality in keeping with the spirit of hope pervading the entire hymn.

The Christian Church is still the most important single phenomenon which human history has to show, stretching beyond the sight of any of us, across the centuries and across the continents; transcending ancient differences of blood and soil, speech and culture; failing and falling often enough, yet through faith rising again, to subdue kingdoms and to work righteousness. Centuries ago, in the name of Christ, the Redeemer, . . . it laid claim to the whole range of our human life from the cradle to the grave. . . .

We are heirs of the Christian ages, wherein that faith has been one of the master-passions of men, a lamp unto their feet and a light unto their path.[10]

[9] Hebrews 12:28 R.S.V.
[10] J. S. Whale, *The Right to Believe* (Charles Scribner's Sons), pp. 51, 52. Used by permission.

THE CHURCH'S ONE FOUNDATION

Samuel J. Stone, 1866

Samuel S. Wesley, 1864
Descant by William Lester Bates, 1930

Descant on 2nd stanza

1. The church's one foun - da - tion Is Je - sus Christ her Lord; She is his new cre -
2. E - lect from eve - ry na - tion, Yet one o'er all the earth, Her char - ter of sal -

a - tion By wa - ter and the word; From heaven he came and sought her To
va - tion One Lord, one faith, one birth; One ho - ly name she bless - es, Par -

be his ho - ly bride; With his own blood he bought her, And for her life he died.
takes one ho - ly food, And to one hope she press - es, With eve - ry grace en - dued.

Descant from H. Augustine Smith, *The New Hymnal for American Youth* (Fleming H. Revell Co.), No. 308. Used by permission.

CHAPTER III

MAKING MUSIC AT HOME

> Day by day, attending the temple together and break-
> ing bread in their homes, they partook of food with glad
> and generous hearts, praising God.[1]

Planned Living

WHAT a picture of balanced life at home and in the church
this diary of the earliest Christians shows! What satisfaction in the
daily practice of religion it reflects! Scan the schedule of your home
routine to observe how the time is budgeted among the activities you
count most important.

The church of our day, in its effort to recover or realize afresh
the "lost radiance of the Christian religion," as L. P. Jacks puts it,
lays special emphasis upon the home as teacher of the "Way,"
guided by the church. Neither church nor home alone can provide
adequate spiritual nurture. Yet the major responsibility belongs
to parents, and it is useless to try to dodge this fact.

> The growth of the appreciation of human values is the essential foundation
> for the growth of the appreciation of God. . . . Children grow into religious
> persons through creative participation in the living of a devoted group. . . .
> The actual valuings of the parents are the educative influences which are at
> work every minute of every day in the lives of their children.[2]

"There's Music in Our House"

We love it! Our equipment is second-string (or should we say "fiddle"), . . .
a thirty-year-old upright piano, . . . a fifteen-year-old radio-phonograph combination, and three shiny, new mouth organs, which we haven't learned to
play yet.

Mom and Dad, though they do nicely singing with the congregation of a Sun-

---

[1] Acts 2:46, 47 R.S.V.

[2] Regina W. Wieman, *The Family Lives Its Religion* (Harper & Bros., 1941), pp.
113, 114, 115. Used by permission.

day morning, know their limitations, and neither Dave nor Jo has had to turn down contracts with the Vienna Choir Boys! We've concluded that it's the music-making that counts and not the finished product, though we've never had a confirmation of this by our neighbors.

Sometimes it's just listening, with other things going on, too. Dressing in the morning may take on a certain flair with the lift of a Strauss waltz or the bristle and blare of a Sousa march, all by the courtesy of one of America's leading railroads which does its best to get Midwest Americans off to a singing start each day. Or maybe it's tackling some long-put-off job on a Saturday afternoon with a broadcast from the Metropolitan filling the house with soaring, golden sound. . . .

Vigorous activity accompanies some of our other listening, too. . . . A favorite record album is Victor's treatment of Tchaikovsky's "Nutcracker Suite" played by the Philadelphia Orchestra under Ormandy. Shoes off, furniture pushed back, we throw ourselves with abandon into our own inimitable interpretations of the haunting music. . . .

Speaking of records, these are among our favorites: "Peter and the Wolf," of course. It's "number one" on our hit parade at the moment. We think there's no finer way to whet a child's fascination for good stories than with really good music. It's a way to become familiar with instruments of the orchestra, too.

A Decca album, "Songs of the African Veld," opened up for us a new treasury of folk music. We are warmed every time we listen to their sly humor and grace as sung by Josef Marais and his company. . . .

A tradition in our family is to waken the household for Christmas morning with the playing of a good recording of much-loved carols. Robert Shaw and the Victor Chorale is our favorite. And for Mom and Dad, among Beethoven's "Seventh Symphony," Marian Anderson's "Great Songs of Faith," and others, are two specials: Helen Traubel's exquisite singing of "Vespers," the musical setting of "Christopher Robin is saying his prayers"; and the lovely Czech soprano, Jarmila Novotna, singing "Cradle Song" in her native tongue. . . . These will always stay with us in a strange and perhaps unimportant way as touching, melodic resolutions of the memories and associations of all fathers and mothers the world around who have ever tucked a sleepy child to bed.

Singing is our best fun, though, around the piano. Dad is an indifferent player, but he can keep rhythm and play enough of the notes to keep the tune recognizable. Best of all our collections, and one we think a family shouldn't be without, is the *Fireside Book of Folksongs* (Simon & Schuster). Here are work songs, ballads, sea chanties, marching songs, carols, hymns, and spirituals. *Come, Let Us Be Joyful,* published by the Cooperative Recreation Service, Delaware, Ohio, gets used a lot, too. . . .

Grace at table is a singing time. We like best "Morning (or noontime or evening) has come," but we're looking to the day when we can sing the round, "For health and strength and daily food."

Piano playing is the frontier in our family musical world. Mom takes lessons and tries to get her practicing in while Jo is taking his nap and Dave is at school. A class in harmony meets every two weeks in our living room. Dave has started simple group lessons at school, and he and his mother have a frequent work-out together. . . .

Come to think of it, music is pretty important in our life as a family. Mostly it's the fun we get out of it. And sometimes it helps us move a little closer to the threshold of the world of the spirit. We felt that way about it during our Christmas Eve family service last year.

Each member of the family made his own special contribution. Dave had learned to play "Silent Night," with one finger, with Dad supplying an unobtrusive but reassuring bass. In the quiet room, the clear, simple melody never sang its message of faith more beautifully. It drifted into silence, and we knew that a gift had been given, and a Presence known in our little company.[3]

Is music as important in your home as in the family so honestly reported on by this father? Write out your own diary for comparison and estimate what your family is gaining or missing from its contacts with music.

1. *Does It Tune Up the Spirit?*

Long before a baby understands words spoken to him, he catches his mother's mood and responds to it in kind. Her voice, pleasing or harsh, is the music that greets the newcomer's ear. The speaking voice has a charm when well used that few utilize for all it is worth. One can detect much of the quality of a family's life by listening in on its conversational tones without even getting the drift of what is said. After a child's mind is able to comprehend language, still he is influenced far more by the emotion behind it than by the word content.

One mother likes to say, "Sing it!" when she overhears her children quarreling. Vainly trying to do that provokes laughter and clears the atmosphere. If we cultivate the habit of singing more and talking less, friction and futile repetition may be decreased. Turn into play by music magic the routine of bathing, dressing, eating, napping. Sing the few necessary words on different tone levels. Watch the mood change when this game is played!

Several times a day the sound of music, filtered into the air that a child breathes, tempers his attitudes and braces his spirit for what occurs. Living interwoven with singing play, work, and worship shapes up according to a purposeful pattern. Music making about

[3] By Oliver Powell from *Children's Religion*. Copyright, The Pilgrim Press. Used by permission of author and publisher.

the house lends buoyancy, to the spirit suggesting that Christians
live there.

2. *Are the Senses Made More Keen?*

Alert are the parents who believe

> Whatever wakes my heart and mind
> Thy presence is, my Lord.[4]

One couple took advantage of the earliest sensory impressions
made upon their daughter to kindle aliveness in several ways:

A baby, Anna, is born. . . . As she develops we give her toys to teach her to
feel, to become color-conscious, to balance, to develop her sense of smell, to gain
acute hearing, . . . to educate the five senses. Those of us who have been awakened
spiritually feel an urge to built up a "plus" sense also—the spiritual or sixth
sense. . . .

Out in the scrubby treetops beside the back door a bird song comes to our
ears. . . . Anna is caught up from her high chair and introduced to the sparrow's
chirp, the robin's spring song, or the mocking bird's meditation.

Again, it is early morning and the baby is wide awake while a still sleepy
parent crawls out to meet her physical needs. Tenderness, joy, expectancy in
the day, expressed through the parent, give the child glimpses of glad things to
come. Dawn may be splashing the clouded sky with bold colors. Through the
window Anna is introduced to color that is registered on her evolving "plus"
sense. Thus mother consciously exposes her baby, day by day, to the rhythms,
the tints, the tones of the universe. . . .

In a thunderstorm is the chance to share much of beauty through sound, the
touch of rain, the fragrance of freshened growth. Mud puddles are places in
which to see mirrored pictures. Flashes of lightning carry messages from the
sky. . . .

In this way as Anna grows older she not only sees, hears, feels, tastes, and
smells, but she joins the great Spirit of the universe in creating. She now has a
storehouse from which to create her own sunsets on large sheets of paper. When
the radio brings an orchestra into her sphere, she translates it into dancing feet.
Her own voice through song or poem, her own fingers through flower arrangement or culinary excursions become an instrument for creative expression.

Even when Anna lives in a city . . . there is music in the huckster's call, in
the ringing of car bells, the honk of auto horns. There is rhythm in whirring
wheels and floating clouds. This exposure to the evidences of continuing creative
activity about her gives an outlet for the real Anna to open herself to God in a
natural way.

[4] From the hymn "O Lord of Life" by George MacDonald. H. Augustine Smith,
The New Hymnal for American Youth (Fleming H. Revell Co.), No. 13.

Things of the spirit, the essence of life, are real to such a child. They are her very own, discovered by her. She doesn't have to hunt for God. He thrills through her being with every organ note. . . . Each flash of lightning quickens her pulse, not to fear, but to joy. The hum of passing traffic gives her a sense of the rhythm that ties the universe together. All her expanding world takes on an expectant quality. She is constantly interpreting her unfolding life in terms of God-consciousness.[5]

Anna is now a young woman trained for full-time service in the Christian Church. Her conviction is, "Because of my home with two parents creative in spirit and my innate abilities, I have an un-quenchable desire to help others to fill their lives more fully with rhythm, color and song! I think we have need of greater kinship with God through these elements." [6]

Having had this upbringing, Anna is awake, as she might not otherwise have been, to joy in simple things. In her present position as Minister of Education in a church she is prepared to lead parents and children to consciousness of the Unseen through music and other agencies.

3. Does It Hold the Group Together?

Singing in unison, agreeing in sound and rhythm, is within the ability of almost every family. By such common action real unity is entered into. How to blend voices into a melodic line has to be learned before individual parts can be put together to form harmony. To match the pitch and pace of another singer is not so easy for a youngster to manage as adults are apt to think. He has to hear much music before he can sing even a fragment of a tune. His first suc-cess is likely to be scored in imitating some repeated sound pattern alone, after, rather than with, another voice.

Think of customs which bind families together. Certain moments in the day are easily marked with appropriate songs. In a home schedule something like this might be recorded: at breakfast sing-ing grace to start the day in a tuneful mood; rhythmic work song to lighten with humor and speed up the chores; interlude between meals, vocal or instrumental, just for fun; a time for listening to something new or hearing an old favorite by way of first-hand per-formance, or record, radio, television, just as one opens a book for refreshment; before going to sleep a song of appreciation for pleasant

[5] Bula C. Wrisley, "Build Up Spiritual Awareness in Your Child," Clear Horizons. VIII, 3, Glenn Clark, ed. Used by permission.
[6] Used by permission.

happenings or the discipline of pain, a hymn of Christain fellowship to include people beyond the circle of kith and kin.

The practicing Christian family feels the need of setting aside
some daily period, however brief, for renewal of life. Imaginative
religion is cultivated as every member takes his turn in putting into
this period what is real from experience, hymn, reading, story, and
other worthful resources. Current incidents of religious significance
and relevance, pictures illuminating Christian thoughts and actions,
surprises of a sort to lend excitement—all can vivify these moments
of togetherness, never to be forgotten. What used to be often formal
or sometimes lifeless "family prayers" may now become with sincere
effort ingenious ways of celebrating what the individuals really live
by.

Agencies outside the church are encouraging systematic habits
of appropriating hymns to daily life at home and in the community
For example, the National Recreation Association, New York City,
puts out a small folder, *Seven Hymns for Everyone, One for Each
Day of the Week*. Their function is to "unite and help us feel what
we have in common." The Federation of Music Clubs provides a
list of twelve hymns, one for each month, for Catholics, Jews, and
Protestants to sing for the strengthening of their religious ties.

Eyes and hands can aid ears and voice in music making. Seeing
the piano played or following the beat of radio or TV music while
clapping the rhythm gives one the feeling of the music's pulse. Hearing and handling toy instruments—sticks, bells, drums, cymbals,
triangles, tambourines—are happy encounters for a child to have
very early. Father, mother, sister, brother, aunt, uncle, grandparent,
guest—one and all are not only eligible to take part in a rhythm band
but they add gaiety to the performance. Anyone who has the urge
to mark time with a tapping foot is ready to join in the fun without previous experience and can contribute to the pleasure of all
concerned.

In this gleeful fashion growing children gain control of their
powers and learn to merge themselves with others in group action.
Only those grown-ups who have been members of this sort of "union"
have any notion of the charming effects it can produce. A family
that knows how to play together is inclined to stay together.[7]

The closer we draw to one another in the home circle, the easier

[7] For helpful suggestions see the pamphlet by Angela Diller and Kate Stearns Page,
How to Teach the Rhythm Band (G. Schirmer, 1930).

40

becomes companionship with our Father. Recognition of this truth is made in the famous hymn, first designed for a table grace, "Now Thank We All Our God." This act of joyous gratitude involves the whole person and the entire family.

4. *What Associations Are Being Set Up?*

College students in a religious education course were asked to trace home and church influences that counted most in shaping their characters. Over a period of years a large collection of papers mentioned almost without exception singing in the family, choir, youth fellowship, or camp. Was this because of the settings in which the experiences were laid, the lasting connections formed, or a combination of many factors?

Family patterns shaped and participated in by all members and group worship with friends under church guidance grip us with tremendous power. Music as a major element attached to pleasant associations lingers in the memory and weaves its spell over one's personality.

Here is a family tradition which was cherished:

> Since our home was founded, Sunday morning has been given over to a program of preparation for our church school and church services. Favorite hymns of the members of the family have been played on our record player while we did our home chores and prepared for church. . . .
>
> Through all the house the air is hushed. . . . Even after he was gone, the words of my father breathed in his Sunday morning grace seemed to echo through the house, "Let us prepare to go into the house of the Lord for worship." [8]

Spontaneous or planned sings around the piano, or without its help, with neighbors and other friends to swell the chorus, may mean a great deal in forming wholesome tastes. Sunday evening was the occasion for one minister's household to do this regularly. A new hymn learned during the week, for daily worship material, built up a memory reserve that was constantly drawn upon. In summer camp, where hymnals were not accessible, they were not missed. With like-minded campers the family gathered in rowboats on a lake for Sunday sings at sunset. They sang remembered hymns, and year after year this inspiring act was renewed. Hence the habit grew

[8] Mabel McKee, "Follow-up for Church Services," *The Christian Home,* May, 1950. Used by permission of the author and publisher.

during recurring seasons to have a firm hold on the affections of the entire camp community of all ages.

No parents using music as an ally in the religious training of their children are capable of meeting their full responsibility alone. They must reach out to agencies which will reinforce young life with strength and beauty.

Both school and church exert dominant controls when boys and girls step outside home limits. Pooling of wisdom results when co-ordination of efforts is planned and pursued. Through parent-teacher meetings of home, church, and school, intelligent co-operation can accomplish much. They can supplement instead of duplicate the musical advantages offered to the children of the entire community. Co-operation in place of competition will require much getting together and adjusting of schedules.

Interchange of helpfulness is easy at Christmas when schools teach carols that children from different religious backgrounds sing with abandon and unanimity. By learning these carols families of Catholic, Jewish, and Protestant faiths can share increasingly "a great joy which will come to *all* the people." [9]

There is no end to the train of associations the Christian family can link up by means of music and the sister arts. Two further hints are: (1) Make the personal element strong by encouraging every one of the household to select an individual song or hymn which becomes his own by memorizing and capturing all he can of its flavor, origin, and authorship. (2) Expand your range of connections by entertaining enthusiasts for music, poetry, and art who will share them interestingly. Older folk and younger near at hand —minister, neighbor, organist, choir director, visitor from out of town—these are acquaintances out of which friends are to be made.[10]

SAMPLING HOMEMADE MUSIC

Tune Up and Speak to Music

1. One parent talks on one tone (that is, *intones*) simple, two-word ideas for the other parent or the child, or both, to repeat. A child will imitate what he hears with another voice or alone. Suggestions attached to music are more likely to be heeded.

[9] Luke 2:10 R.S.V.
[10] Consult for inspiration and example Annis Duff, *Bequest of Wings,* Chapter IX, "Music My Rampart" (The Viking Press).

42

Greeting, Signal, Suggestion

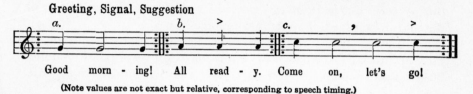

Good morn - ing! All read - y. Come on, let's go!

(Note values are not exact but relative, corresponding to speech timing.)

2. In singing conversation parent and child make up their parts as they speak on one tone of medium pitch. Continue and develop as long as interest lasts.

Question and Answer
(Parent)   *(Child)*

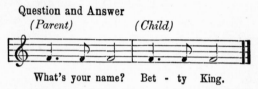

What's your name? Bet - ty King.

3. Exclaim on high, medium, or low tone words conveying different moods. Try each on three pitches to find which one expresses the feeling best. This singing speech fits into a daily routine at many points once it is adopted.

Expressing Moods on Different Pitch Levels

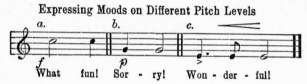

What fun! Sor - ry! Won - der - ful!

Chanting

1. *Chant* on two or more tones (the earliest kind of Christian song, most elemental of tunes). Re-create the joyful spirit of the "Sursum Corda" ("Lift up your hearts"), sung continuously since the fourth century. Clothe it in a chant of your own making. First, intone on a pitch in the middle register to set rhythm and pace. Then sing on that pitch all the words except the most important words which move to higher or lower tone, as seems right. When the call and response patterns, after experiment, have been accepted, they might serve as a table grace or invitation to prayer or singing.

Two-tone Tunes
(One Voice)   *(Other Voices)*

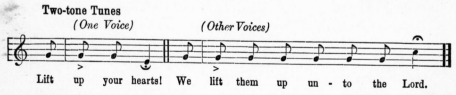

Lift up your hearts! We lift them up un - to the Lord.

2. See what can be done with a poetic line from the Psalms when any number of scale tones are put into a freely moving chant. Each individual try is repeated by the group. The one that wins the most approval is picked out on the piano, written down, and becomes later a starting point for further chant improvising.

Six-tone Tune

O sing un - to the Lord a new song!

Develop Sense of Rhythm

1. Make bodily response to ordinary sounds—striking of the hour, for instance, beating time to singing or playing the piano (or to records or radio music). Step on tip-toe, tap lightly, etc.

2. Play toy instruments of the kinds heard in band and orchestra —triangle, drum, cymbals, tambourine (percussion, striking movements). Count "one-two," accenting "one" every time. Keeping time with another person is fundamental to all teamwork.

During the playing of these two Schumann numbers interpret the rhythmic patterns by using any of the above ideas or following suggestions the music makes to you.

A Story

"Album for the Young"
Robert Schumann

Don't hurry

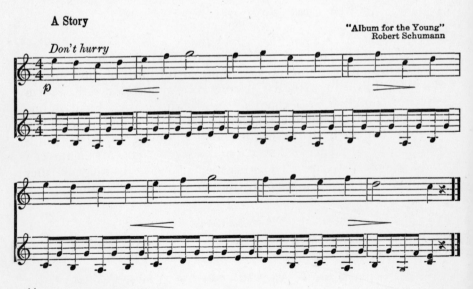

A Hymn

"Album for the Young"
Robert Schumann

Harmonizing

1. Listen to and reproduce harmonies by cultivating ability to hear upper and lower tones that blend rather than jar the sensibilities. Such perceptions train one to recognize and delight in tonal values. Eventually this skill takes a family into round singing, two, three, or four parts, according to the size of the circle. No other exercise shows better what co-operation produces in place of competition. How surprising it is that one melody can be transformed into harmony when it is treated as a round!

2. Listen to chord playing. On syllable "Ah!" sound upper, then lower tone, or tones, in order singly. Divide into parts and sing two, three, or four tones at the same time to produce a harmonious chord.

Examples:

Each individual improvises his own tune, out of one, three, five, eight of the scale, after hearing the four tones played, while all sing at the same time their different tunes.

Announce Chord:

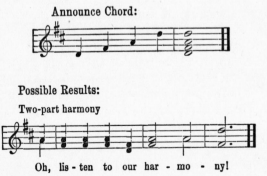

Possible Results:

Two-part harmony

Oh, lis - ten to our har - mo - ny!

Three-part harmony

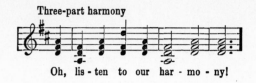

Oh, lis - ten to our har - mo - ny!

Four-part harmony

Oh, lis - ten to our har - mo - ny!

Tune: "Brother John" round, with words adapted to getting together for a sing. (Make up your own version.)

Original words—each line repeated:

> Are your sleeping,
> Brother John?
> Morning bells are ringing:
> Ding, ding, dong!

Time for sing - ing, Time for sing - ing; Oh, give thanks! Oh, give thanks!

Serve the Lord with glad-ness; Serve the Lord with glad-ness; Sing for joy! Sing for joy!

"The Tie That Binds"

1. Exchange memories of singing times at home that united "hearts in Christian love." Is "O God, Our Help" one of the hymns?

2. What modern ones bind together your household today?

3. To "be bound in the bundle of the living in the care of the Lord your God" [11] is a union that music can strengthen. Elect by popular vote some hymn, new or old, which the family, or this class, chooses to become specially its own. One written originally for family use, including all ages, the past and present, all caught up in an act of courtesy toward God, is "Now Thank We All Our God."

[11] I Samuel 25:29 R.S.V.

NOW THANK WE ALL OUR GOD

Martin Rinkart, c. 1630
Tr. Catherine Winkworth, 1858

Johann Crüger, 1647
Adapted by Felix Mendelssohn, 1840

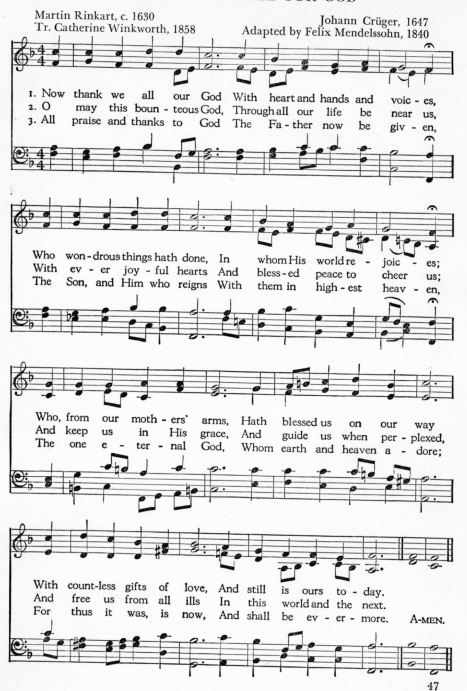

1. Now thank we all our God With heart and hands and voic - es,
2. O may this boun - teous God, Through all our life be near us,
3. All praise and thanks to God The Fa - ther now be giv - en,

Who won - drous things hath done, In whom His world re - joic - es;
With ev - er joy - ful hearts And bless - ed peace to cheer us;
The Son, and Him who reigns With them in high - est heav - en,

Who, from our moth - ers' arms, Hath blessed us on our way
And keep us in His grace, And guide us when per - plexed,
The one e - ter - nal God, Whom earth and heaven a - dore;

With count-less gifts of love, And still is ours to - day.
And free us from all ills In this world and the next.
For thus it was, is now, And shall be ev - er - more. A-MEN.

47

CHAPTER IV

KNOWING THE MUSIC OF OUR CHURCH

My heart is ready, ready, O God, for song and melody.[1]
O thou Eternal, . . . all our days we shall make music
at thy house unto thy praise.[2]

THE story of tuning music to the voice of worship in the Christian Church is a live and fascinating one. Learning to select from this story certain chapters that trace its forms, as it changed from age to age to fit new experiences, is a "must" for music leaders. Knowing where to look for the various expressions that "speak to our condition" and urge us forward to shape true instruments of devotion is the duty and privilege of all those who are in charge of the musical program. The first form in point of view of history is:

1. Plain Song

This type of music is described as:

The most complete artistic treasure bequeathed to us by antiquity. . . . It is the world's primary treasure of wholly artistic melody. . . . [It] uplifts the mind into a perennially vital expression of worship directed to the one true God, as revealed through his eternal Son in words inspired by the Holy Spirit.[3]

For hundreds of years Christians employed plain song as their only worship music, and they have chanted it continuously up to the present along with the newer forms which have been created. It is "plain" because all can sing it in unison in a flowing melody that conforms to the thought expressed, uninterrupted by musical accent, and not dependent upon instrumental accompaniment. Since the end of the sixth century plain song has been known as Gregorian Chant, named after Pope Gregory who perfected and systematized this special art of chanting. Canon Winfred Douglas, a plain song

---

[1] Psalm 57:7 Moffatt.
[2] Isaiah 38:20 Moffatt.
[3] Winfred Douglas, *Church Music in History and Practice* (Charles Scribner's Sons, 1937) , pp. 28, 29. Used by permission.

authority, states these principles, among others, which he believes make this type of church song distinctive and valid for today's singing:

The music . . . was sung to the praise of God, and not to man.

The music was an integral part of each service, not a decorative addition. The sung worship was not individualistic prayer, but the voice of the whole church.

The congregation was supplied with refrains and with simple melodies suited to their vocal ability. For the choir, there were more elaborate compositions, in some of which skilled solo cantors found opportunity to exercise their best powers in God's praise.

The music was subordinate to the text. The musical style was purely religious, and unrelated to that of secular music.[4]

When you search your hymnals, you will find easy plain song chants set to Bible passages pertinent to a number of present worship demands and of enduring beauty. Through them singers realize the truth that "all the earth doth worship thee, the Father everlasting," as they join in the very same music that Christendom, almost from its beginning, has found to be a direct line, so to speak, with the Eternal. Not to know about, or to neglect the use of, plain song is to be cut off from a portion of every Christian's birthright.

A COLLEGE STUDENT'S CHOICE OF PLAIN SONG: "DIVINUM MYSTERIUM"

In the German University of Rostock there was a young Finn, Theodoric Petri (Didrik Pedersen) in 1582, who collected from his fellow students songs and hymns which he published as a school hymnal when he was a sophomore. Called *Piae Cantiones,* then a common title for religious songs, it became a very famous book. Numbers from it are still used widely. One of these was the already two-hundred-year-old plain song tune "Divinum Mysterium." The hymnal found its way into the hands of the British Minister at Stockholm, Sweden. Taking it to his native country, he gave it to Thomas Helmore, who with Dr. John Mason Neale introduced it with a Latin hymn translation, into English hymnbooks. The Latin hymn for Christmas, joined to this tune, was written by Prudentius, a Spaniard, the earliest of Christian authors who was a genuine poet. By way of this international chain comes the song which publishes the good news of the Incarnation. Starting out from Italy the plain song music went on tour to Germany, was published by a Finn,

[4] *Ibid.,* pp. 27, 28.

taken by a British Minister to men who united it with a Latin hymn by a Spanish author, then translated it into English. From England the hymn and tune were relayed to American hymnals, where they are sung here six hundred years later. Observe this as evidence that the true ecumenical church has been building our hymnals for centuries.

A more familiar example, sung at Christmas, is the haunting plain song melody, "Veni Emmanuel," set to the old Latin hymn done into English, "O Come, O Come, Emmanuel." A simple adaptation of plain chant very generally known is the tune, "Hamburg," for "When I Survey the Wondrous Cross," adapted by our American composer Lowell Mason.

Let this kind of musical speaking lift to a higher plane parts of the service ordinarily spoken. A call to singing, "O Praise Ye the Lord" [5]; a prayer response, perhaps the "Lord's Prayer"; a transition from one act of worship to another which is made with more ease by music—these are places in a service order where chanting is a particularly useful form of church song.

Children and adults have made the chant a take-off for improvising their own modern tunes to verses that lend themselves to responsive treatment. "Thou hast put gladness in my heart" [6]; "This is the Lord's doing; it is marvelous in our eyes" [7]; "Oh that men would praise the Lord for his goodness, and for his wonderful works to the children of men!" [8] are provocative Psalm lines to try out for this kind of melody-making. Interpreting their meanings with spoken thoughts which follow the chanted quotation opens up a productive experience in group praying.

Plain song, one doorway to the wonderful world of Christian song, can be entered any day in the year; but religious education requires that it be not passed by. Through "Divinum Mysterium" is a lovely entrance into the wonder of the Advent and Christmas season as it gives us a glimpse into its significance.

2. Folk Song (Carol)

As plain song grew into a more and more elaborate art, it demanded diligent practice on the part of choirs dedicated to its mastery. For that reason the responsibility for singing was transferred

---

[5] Edith Lovell Thomas, *Singing Worship* (Abingdon-Cokesbury Press), No. 28.
[6] Psalm 4:7 A.S.V.
[7] Psalm 118:23 K.J.V.
[8] Psalm 107:8 K.J.V.

gradually to trained voices, and the congregation was reduced to silence. The balance had to be restored somehow, and one of the ways it came about was through the folk song, often a carol, the outgrowth of a ring dance.

St. Francis in the thirteenth century, loving to sing, was spoken of as the "Lark" and the "Troubadour of God." He is said to have been the first to dramatize the Nativity, to revive in the hearts of the people the love of Christ, grown cold through formal ritual or forgetting. He inspired his own Italian people to sing the gospel story to simple folk tunes. Realism and gaiety came into religion, as people merged song with living, through the medium of rhythmic carols. The carol as a dance was transformed into a festive celebration of religion, not only for Christmas, but many times the whole year round.

A JOYFUL OLD CAROL: "IN DULCI JUBILO"

This fourteenth-century Christmas carol according to a legend was sung by angels to a devout monk, Henry Suso, inducing him to dance with them involuntarily. The words appear amusing to us as they mix languages, "macaronic" style; but they reflect the period out of which they came, when the vernacular was being substituted for Latin. Switching back and forth between the old and the new languages was a very human attempt to hold on to the best that was known while accepting something novel.

It was sung at the newly opened Moravian Mission in Pennsylvania on Christmas Eve, 1741, under the leadership of Count Zinzendorf, who had so strongly influenced the Wesleys. On the same night another carol, "Not Jerusalem; rather Bethlehem," gave the name to the new settlement, and the present city. There, on September 14, four years later, the old mission diary records that *"In dulci jubilo"* was sung simultaneously in thirteen languages, European and Indian, accompanied by an orchestra. Surely the macaronic trend could go no further! [9]

This carol, loved by numberless carolers, has a way of turning up in popular books scattered throughout many lands—in Luther's last hymnal in 1545 in German, in *Piae Cantiones* in 1582 in Swedish, and in *Carols for Christmastide* in 1853 by John Mason Neale with his original English words, "Good Christian Men, Rejoice," to mention only three.

[9] Winfred Douglas, *op. cit.*, pp. 203, 204.

The rollicking six-four measure and short, lilting lines appeal to all kinds of people, just what old and young like to sing at home, something to salute neighbors with in street caroling, and to infuse into a church service a childlike quality of merriment.

The singing of carols is increasing as a good custom among us, and perhaps the candlelight and other carol services are more enjoyed by choirs and congregations than any other musical medium. In our hymnals the number of tunes from folk-song sources is growing larger, and we are thereby blessed. The Silesian air for "Fairest Lord Jesus," and the "Netherlands Folk Song" with "We Gather Together" or "We Praise Thee, O God," are two which usually win nearly one hundred per cent response from old and young, whenever they are announced.

English hymnals have appropriated the folk-carol type of song for worship with such good results that American books are following their lead with excellent choices from this field.

3. The Golden Age of Church Music

MUSIC OF MANY MELODIES: PALESTRINA'S "VICTORY"

The sixteenth century will always be remembered for the creation of marvelous church music which weaves many melodies into one composition, giving to each voice a thread of a different hue and making a design of indescribable tonal beauty. From among several great musicians of this era Palestrina stands out as a superb composer and master of choirs in Rome. He left about seven hundred works for the church, imperishable in grandeur. Hearing well done presentations of this literature by choirs in church, at concerts, or on records is a real part of the religious culture of every child of the church. For demonstration of the heights to which music can ascend when guided by religion the work of Palestrina and his contemporaries is indeed revealing.

Our hymnals give us a chance to become members of Palestrina's choir, in one unique number. His music, usually so far beyond our powers that it must be brought to us by skilled voices, is in the tune "Victory," made possible for us all to sing with the Easter hymn, "The strife is o'er."

From the 1591 music for the "Gloria Patri" by Palestrina, Dr. William Henry Monk in 1861 adapted this example of the golden age of church music to a hymn tune in which any and all congregations can glory. The "alleluias" to begin and end with were written by Dr. Monk.

Easter is well celebrated when full musical resources of the people in the pews as well as in the chancel are drawn upon. Men's and women's lower and upper ranges should occasionally be heard in their natural registers from the congregation, to bring out the melodies that lie below the soprano level. Impressive as unison is, congregational music done in four parts with each part supplying its melody makes a most powerful musical speech. The rehearsing required would be a worthy and rewarding Lenten exercise for any congregation.

The Easter text has been through a series of translations beginning in Latin with an unknown author and ending in Francis Pott's English version in 1861.

Ask your choir to render unaccompanied Palestrina's "Adoramus te" to usher you into the lofty Presence where you can bear witness with Isaiah, "I saw the Lord . . . high and lifted up!" [10] Although repeated often after centuries of steady wear, its radiance is not dulled.

The literature of the golden age is too extensive to pursue here, but with the guidance of your choir each year you should become constantly better acquainted with it.

4. German Chorale

CONGREGATIONAL SONG: "LIEBSTER JESU"

Back and forth the pendulum swings in worship music, now touching the choir's side and then returning to the people's. Happy the church that is able to keep the rhythmic movement at an even pulse so that both sides fully function. The proportion of energy, intelligence, and enthusiasm contributed by each bears continual watching and directing. The church of the past should teach us the tragedy of the choir holding the balance of power. Time and again the rights of the congregation have been neglected or virtually usurped, and new procedures have had to be put into effect. The Reformation freed the people from restraints that had limited their participation in the musical service of worship, when the choir practically monopolized the office, by opening up a new channel for them.

The emancipated layman found in the general hymn a symbol as well as an agent of the assertion of his new rights and privileges in the Gospel. The people's

[10] Isaiah 6:1 A.S.V.

song of early Protestantism has therefore a militant ring. It marks an epoch no less significantly than Luther's ninety-five theses and the Augsburg Confession. It was a sort of spiritual *Triumphlied,* proclaiming to the universe that the day of spiritual emancipation had dawned. . . .

The melodies to which the hymns of Luther and his followers were set became the foundation of a musical style which is the one school worthy to be placed beside the Italian Catholic music of the sixteenth century.[11]

The Palestrina selection just noted was chosen from this latter music.

What number shall be lifted out of the vast collection of German chorales which not only revolutionized the service of worship but extended far beyond it to change the course of the development of the whole art of music?

"Liebster Jesu" ("Blessed Jesus") , an exquisite one, was composed by Johann R. Ahle in 1664 for a hymn beginning with the same words, the convenient method the Germans have of naming tunes. The hymn was to be sung on Sunday just before the sermon. Worship as fellowship, direct access to God for the individual, and reverence for the Bible as the revelation of God to each human being are convictions of the new Protestant religion reflected in this hymn.

A prayerful mood pervades the quiet melody, clear-cut in outline and purposeful, an ideal tune for congregational singing. A choir or quartet, singing the second stanza in four parts, preserves a pause for the congregation to note more carefully the beauty of the harmony and to let the meaning of the confession of faith sink in.

Another chorale which challenges hearty singing is "Lobet den Herren" ("Praise to the Lord, the Almighty") , conceived in a mood of rejoicing. For children and youth especially "Come Together, Let Us Sing," by Bach,[12] is a clear call to worship through joyous music.

The foundation for a sturdy character is laid when one's singing experience is built on the German chorale as one of its elements. Singers thus grounded have withstood many crises which would overpower weaker souls.

The treasure of grand chorales which Protestants possess has come to us through the Lutheran tradition and is becoming more generally appreciated throughout all denominations with the years. Choirs are using them with greater value as they know them more

---

[11] Edward Dickinson, *Music in the History of the Western Church* (Charles Scribner's Sons) , pp. 224, 225, 226. Used by permission.

[12] E. C. Schirmer Music Co., publishers.

intimately. Every year more of this kind of substantial music is being taught to children to their advantage. The chorales are being sought by those who appreciate their vigor, majesty, and the impression they convey of a religion that is dignified and upstanding.

For Johann Sebastian Bach, the father of Protestant church music, chorales were an inexhaustible mine where he found themes for a host of compositions, instrumental as well as choral. Knowing chorales, therefore, equips one with a key which unlocks a large store of the world's greatest music for organ—the cantatas, oratorios, passions, and other forms of choral music.

5. Psalm Tune

Parallel to the Lutheran strain of hymnic music runs another that we prize greatly and put to generous use wherever Christians meet for worship. From this vein we recall possibly the most popular of all sacred tunes, "Old 100th," bequeathed to us by our psalm-singing fathers. They passed the psalm tune on through the Reformed branch of the family, stemming primarily from John Calvin and his celebrated musical editor, the French composer Louis Bourgeois, as they worked together in Geneva, Switzerland.

The chaste simplicity and solemnity of "Old 100th" and kindred settings for metrical versions of the Psalms have kept the whole world singing for four hundred years. An English counterpart is noble old "St. Anne," one of the sublime congregational numbers which is adequate to crucial times in history, when, as on V-E and V-J days, an interfaith gathering asserts its trust in the one unfailing Source of help. Isaac Watts wrote the incomparable paraphrase of the ninetieth psalm, long linked to "St. Anne," "O God, our help in ages past." William Croft, to whom the music is attributed, ranks high among those to whom worshipers everywhere turn for music that gives them permanent satisfaction.

Psalm singing was deeply loved by our Pilgrim fathers when they developed free worship in the Plymouth settlement. They sang from the Ainsworth Psalter, *The Booke of Psalms: Englished both in Prose and Metre,* named for the man who prepared it for them when they lived in Holland. Of the music he says, "Tunes for the Psalms I find none set of God; so that each people is to use the most grave, decent and comfortable manner of singing that they know." He took tunes from other English psalters and the "gravest and easiest tunes of the French and Dutch psalmes." One of the psalm tunes (the melody line) as printed by Ainsworth with the version of the ninety-fifth psalm could be fittingly sung on Thanksgiving. If the Pilgrims used it on their first Thanksgiving in November, 1621, imagine for what they were thankful! When referring to "rock of our health" they could count only 55 of the 101 voyagers who had come ashore from the Mayflower the year before. Starvation, sickness, and death had afflicted them. Had it not been for the Indians, who gave them seed corn and showed them how to raise it, all of them might have perished. Were they thinking gratefully of the good Chief Massasoit and the ninety Indian guests with whom they made a pact of peace, feasting for three days, when they sang, "Let us present his face with thanksgiving"?

The Indians held the Great Spirit in reverence as the giver of growing things and all wonders. Feeling themselves at home among the beauties of the universe, they learned some of its secrets. For the knowledge they shared the Pilgrims could indeed offer gratitude.

The psalm tunes were too beautiful to be confined strictly to Psalms. Many of them are mated with hymns of later origin in the newest hymnals, where you come upon superior samples, for example, "Old 124th" in its shortened form, "Toulon," [13] and "Old 113th" ("Lucerne"), [14] a favorite of John Wesley's.

6. Newer Trends in Our Hymnals

Changing from one type of music to another and introducing hymns in place of or in addition to the words of psalms have not been done without opposition. Men have even been sent to prison for trying to promote new forms of worship song. Yet each of the five classes of church music thus far noted has enriched immeasurably the expressive possibilities which are ours because of the vision and courage of musical pioneers. Our newest and best hymnals include all these varieties and show a more and more ecumenical trend. In hymnals, as in no other connection, we have a real union of the nations and all types of religious faith. We take heart in the ringing testimony that

> In Christ *now* meet both East and West,
> In him meet South and North.[15]

[13] Set to Denis Wortman's "God of the prophets! bless the prophets' sons," in *The Hymnal* (Protestant Episcopal) , No. 220.

[14] *The Methodist Hymnal*, No. 513.

[15] John Oxenham, "In Christ There Is No East or West."

This was not always so. Plain song, psalm tune, or other variety was in different eras a sole musical mode of worship. Although the music from all sources now collected in a single book is one in function, to "make His praise glorious," each nation and sect has put its distinctive accent on what it has brought to the whole. Three of these accents may serve to point up trends seen in more modern tunes cited from three distinctive origins.

EMPHASIS ON REALITY AND QUALITY: ENGLISH COMPOSERS

Ralph Vaughan Williams and Martin Shaw, eminent English composers and editors of superior hymnals, have been concerned to do away with weak, sentimental sacred music. One substitute is arrangements of forthright folk songs, singable, and suited to various groups. These musicians have not been content to print them merely but have devoted much time to teaching congregations to sing them with sincerity. Much that hitherto was deemed outside the province of worship because of its secular association has been made sacred by nobler use, a natural medium for uttering the best within the human heart. The body of this spontaneous folk melody is large and promising. It is directed not only toward adults, but much of it is adapted to young people's and children's interests and abilities.

"Royal Oak" is a traditional English melody, first used as a hymn tune and printed on a sheet for community singing by Martin Shaw, to which is sung "All things bright and beautiful," a child's hymn.[16] Its brisk movement and charming air are like a fresh breeze in contrast to the stale atmosphere of poor tunes children are too apt to identify with "Sunday school songs."

Training congregations to exert themselves heart, soul, mind, and strength calls for new compositions as well as the tested and familiar. The choir should broaden its understanding of the significance of hymn tunes and how people can be helped to sing them with profit. This creative task has been one of the outstanding services of the above mentioned and other talented musicians of the modern English school of church composers.

"Sine Nomine," [17] one of Ralph Vaughan Williams' own tunes, is challenging to choristers and people alike. "For all the saints who from their labors rest" is the hymn that he felt demanded rousing music, since it pays honor to the memory of the host of those who have marked out the shining way of religion for us. The treatment

[16] *The Hymnal* (Protestant Episcopal) , No. 311.
[17] *The Methodist Hymnal*, No. 527.

of the long hymn of eight stanzas is varied by unison and four-part singing. Fully written out music and words cover two pages. A solo voice can take some lines, and the "alleluia's" are then done by choir and congregation. Certain stanzas are impressively rendered by the choir in harmony. The last stanza concentrates all forces in one great unison chorus of pew and chancel singers for contrast and triumphant effect.

PARTICIPATION WITH POWER: WELSH TUNES

Distinguished by their love of good music and resonant part singing, Welsh congregations have much to teach churches that have let congregational singing languish or have never cultivated it wholeheartedly. The entire congregation does the singing, usually without benefit of choir. The more recent any church hymnal is, the larger is the place accorded to Welsh hymn tunes. Upon full participation depends their power to stir people to the depths. The virile, rugged rhythms, strong melodies, and wide ranging harmonies of Welsh tunes, like "Cwm Rhondda" [18] and "Meirionydd," [19] have no parallel in music poured forth from other peoples. The valiant element in them is one desperately demanded in the growing of stalwart Christians today.

IMAGINATION AND DARING IN AMERICAN CHURCH TUNES

That which is most precious is a long time coming into being. The tunes that we hold in affection are probably those we have known longest. But however old they are to us, once they were new. The most noteworthy music is improved by age, but its quality of aliveness makes it always new. How then is worship music to be something more than a gift from the past which we appropriate and benefit ourselves thereby? Each generation must give account of its talents in terms of its own experiences in order to avoid being a parasite on the past, to make its own growth possible, and to share with future generations its intimations of eternal life.

Whether fresh creations will be accepted and become of permanent value or not, no one can know. But the urge to write music, such as hymn tunes, will not be denied; and the desire to design a better vehicle for "commerce with God" ever drives men to try out new inventions.

[18] *The Methodist Hymnal,* No. 279.
[19] *Ibid.,* No. 454.

Our own country is very young when compared with the years it takes to make a new kind of worship song and have it adopted by Christians privately and publicly. Nevertheless as we look back over the brief sacred music history of our country, we discover that men of imagination and daring have been instituting changes for the better in our singing.

Lowell Mason, the father of American church music, changed the deadening habit of "lining out" psalms into singing "Joy to the world" to his inspiring tune "Antioch," arranged from Handel themes. Composing, arranging, editing song and hymnbooks, he was also the first teacher of music as a study to receive credit in the public school. He organized and trained children's and adult choirs, conducted conferences for teachers and advanced the cause of good music in church and school. He found worship music inconceivably poor and remade it into kinds that we would find hard to do without today. Quiz yourselves on how many of Mason's hymn tunes you can name quickly. Look in the composers' index in your hymnal for well-known tunes you overlooked.

Horatio W. Parker, educated in this country and in Europe, composer, organist, choirmaster, professor of music at Yale University, an editor of the Episcopal hymnal, said, "We need not more tunes, but better ones, attaining a higher standard of musical worth and dignity." He came at a time when the gospel song was popular and frequently displaced the more churchly and longer lasting hymn tune. This adventure of raising standards he embarked upon, creating his "Pro Patria," [20] among many excellent tunes. That well interprets the daring spirit of modern missions, as pictured in the text that goes with it, "Heralds of Christ, who bear the King's commands." A vigorous march, a clarion call to action, and a wide-sweeping melody, supported by spirited harmony, combine to stir youth and their elders to enlist in the Christian crusade.

H. Augustine Smith, for a half century directing choirs, making youth and church hymnals, and conducting courses in church music and worship, awakened churches to a concern for Christian education through music. Dr. Smith pioneered in capturing for young people the arresting music and poetry of today's best composers and authors. He culled from many original experiments illustrations of freer kinds of tunes and newer thoughts to induce worship.

[20] H. Augustine Smith, *The New Hymnal for American Youth,* No. 258.

Among the examples of freer forms of tunes and texts these are cited:

1. Breaking away from the usual four- or eight-line hymn tune structures, to accompany the blank verse of the poem "To Every Man," George Henry Day writes "Decision." [21] To be sung in unison, with an accompaniment which deviates from the melodic line, it dramatizes the thought content. John Oxenham, author of the text, deals with the choice everyone must make between the high, low, and in-between paths of life which his soul will take. Dr. Day's music distinguishes the emotional states of indecision, drifting, and definite choosing, moving through the minor and chromatic changes until it issues in the resolute major key. Like the "through composed" art song of Schubert, colored by different shades of meaning in the lyrics, this is a medium which gives a brief sacred song a greater range of expression.

2. Another instance of vivid music from the same book is Leroy B. Campbell's "Hosanna," [22] a Palm Sunday number, effective as a processional. By means of the Dorian, an early church mode, we are transported to the far away and long ago scene of the triumphal entry into Jerusalem. We shout and move with the multitude in unison song. The many-voiced chords of the accompaniment have four to nine tones each and pack the scene with throngs of people. The event is made so real to the singer that in the language of the Katharine Lee Bates poem we offer "ourselves thy branches" even as the palm branches were first presented to the "Lord of Light."

Song-hymns like these provide young and older singers in church school and choir with a climate where they can express themselves more fully and therein grow into more mature Christians. New ways of singing together are as essential to growth as is the teaching of older and more usual modes which have been made their own. The province of the leader is to secure for them a balance of old and new musical diet and to include all elements with which to meet life with adequacy. Your selection will differ very likely from mine. However, so long as each development of the church's heritage of song is wisely utilized, our children will receive the bounty that belongs to them.

[21] *Ibid.*, No. 232.
[22] *Ibid.*, No. 114.

TUNES TESTED IN CHRISTIAN EXPERIENCE

Do you find in the tunes that follow what has made them survive?
What other classifications and samples would you include to round
out a dozen tunes you believe everyone should know?

These six are but a preface to choices you personally would rank
first in importance:

1. Plain Song: "Divinum Mysterium."
2. Folk Song (Carol): "In Dulci Jubilo."
3. The Golden Age of Church Music: "Victory."
4. German Chorale: "Liebster Jesu."
5. Psalm Tune: From the "Ainsworth Psalter."
6. Newer Trends in Our Hymnals: "Pro Patria."

1. *Plain Song*

OF THE FATHER'S LOVE BEGOTTEN

Prudentius, 348-413
Tr. John Mason Neale, 1854   "Divinum Mysterium"
Smoothly, not too slow   13th C. Plainsong, Mode V

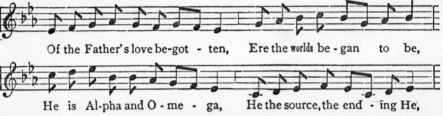

Of the Father's love be-got - ten, Ere the worlds be - gan to be,

He is Al-pha and O - me - ga, He the source, the end - ing He,

Of the things that are, that have . . . . been, And that fu - ture

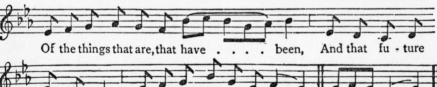

years shall see, Ev- er-more and ev - er - more! A - men.

The Hymnal (Protestant Episcopal), 1940, No. 20.

2. *Folk Song* (*Carol*)

IN DULCI JUBILO

German, 14th Century
Harm. by Bartholomew Gesius, 1601

In Dulci Jubilo = in sweet rejoicing
In presepio = in a manger
Matris in gremio = in the lap of his mother
Alpha es et O = thou art Alpha (A) and O (Omega) first and last
    letters of Greek alphabet, that is, the beginning and the end
O Jesu parvule = O little Jesus
O puer optime = O boy best of all
O princeps gloriae = O prince of glory
Trahe me post te = draw me after thee

3. *The Golden Age of Church Music*

Hymn tune: "Victory" from Palestrina's "Gloria Patri"

To taste the individual flavors of the melodies that are woven together to make the four-part harmony sing: (1) In unison alto, tenor, and bass parts in succession, omitting "alleluias." (2) Divide into two groups and make a duet of alto and tenor parts, tenor and bass, and alto and bass. (3) Sing four parts together.

THE STRIFE IS O'ER

Tr. from the Latin, 1695, by
Francis Pott, 1861

Palestrina, 1588
adapted with Alleluias by
William H. Monk, 1861

Al - le - lu - ia! Al - le - lu - ia! Al - le - lu - ia! 1. The strife is
2. The pow'rs of
3. The three sad
4. Lord, by the

o'er, the bat - tle done; The vic - to - ry of life is won;
death have done their worst, But Christ their le - gions hath dis - persed;
days have quick - ly sped; He ris - es glo - rious from the dead:
stripes which wound - ed Thee, From death's dread sting Thy ser - vants free,

The song of tri - umph has be - gun. Al - le - lu - ia!
Let shouts of ho - ly joy out - burst. Al - le - lu - ia!
All glo - ry to our ris - en Head! Al - le - lu - ia!
That we may live and sing to Thee. Al - le - lu - ia! A - MEN.

4. *German Chorale*

BLESSED JESUS, AT THY WORD

Tobias Clausnitzer
Tr. by Catherine Winkworth

"Liebster Jesu"
Johann R. Ahle

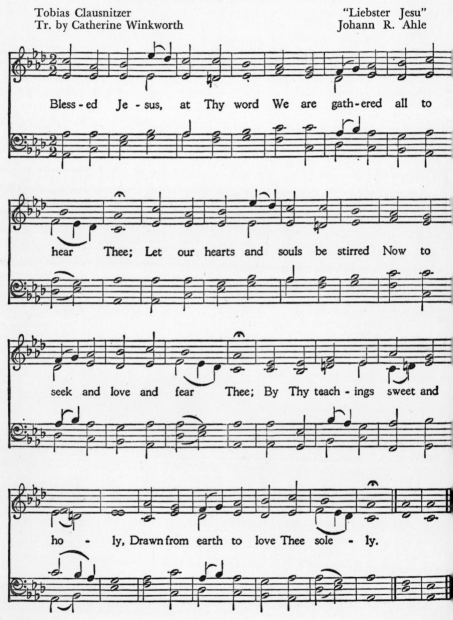

Bless-ed Je-sus, at Thy word We are gath-ered all to

hear Thee; Let our hearts and souls be stirred Now to

seek and love and fear Thee; By Thy teach-ings sweet and

ho - ly, Drawn from earth to love Thee sole - ly.

5. Psalm Tune

THANKSGIVING PSALM

Part of the 95th Psalm turned into   Tune from the Ainsworth Psalter, 1612
metre by Henry Ainsworth   Harmonized by E. L. T.

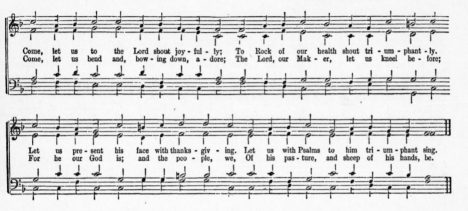

Missing Links

Supply what you think is missing from above classifications to round out examples of what is important to a satisfying knowledge of the church's musical art.

You would probably wish to have represented the vast library of organ literature—the kind of music that silences a congregation on entering a sanctuary and encourages reverence. Perhaps you would mention some selections that induce several contrasting devotional moods. Can you name their composers? To what ages might they be suggestive? Are any of them adaptable to piano?

Are there certain types of piano compositions which should be heard in church school for purposes of listening, study, or worship? What illustrations can you cite?

Should a child form acquaintance with the larger sacred choral works as part of his Christian education? If so, what quotations would you star from the minimum essential works?

To what anthems, if any, would you introduce a child to help him understand and enjoy the choir's musical ministry? In what ways can this introduction be made of most value to him?

What other links are required by one who would gain a working knowledge of the best the church has to offer her children in music?

6. *Newer Trends in Our Hymnals*

HERALDS OF CHRIST

"Pro Patria"

Laura S. Copenhaver, 1921   Horatio W. Parker, 1894

1. Her - alds of Christ who bear the King's com - mands, Im - mor - tal tid - ings
2. Thro' des - ert ways, dark fen and deep mo - rass, Thro' jun - gles, slug - gish
3. Where once the twist - ing trail in dark - ness wound, Let march - ing feet and
4. Lord, give us faith and strength the road to build, To see the prom - ise

in your mor - tal hands, Pass on and car - ry swift the news ye
seas, and moun-tain pass, Build ye the road, and fal - ter not, nor
joy - ous song re - sound; Where burn the fun - eral pyres and cen - sers
of the day ful - filled, When war shall be no more and strife shall

bring, Make straight, make straight the high - way of the King.
stay, Pre - pare a - cross the earth the King's high - way.
swing, Make straight, make straight the high - way of the King.
cease Up - on the high - way of the Prince of Peace. A-MEN.

Used by permission of Mrs. Ralph B. Semler.

CHAPTER V

SELECTING AND INTRODUCING SONGS AND HYMNS

The fineness which a hymn or psalm affords
Is when the soul unto the lines accords.[1]

DELVING into the stream of church music and taking from it the richest deposits it has for us today is but one phase of our task, though an immensely important one. What shall we sing about and what music shall we sing are companion questions we must answer. Choosing this from that must be constantly done in the light of better understanding of the age we teach, new knowledge attained, and larger vision of possibilities to be experienced.

To become mature Christians we grow little by little to love God and our neighbors with heart, mind, soul, and strength—Jesus' definition of what really matters. The building of these right relationships in emotion, thought, word, and action is powerfully helped or retarded by what and how we sing. For we put into song the feelings, ideas, imagination, and hopes which shape the persons we become. We make singing a direct means of connecting ourselves with others in fellowship as we take part in worship and celebrate occasions of high moment.

What governs the selection of songs and hymns will be determined by what serves the singers best and what ministers to their growth in Christian character.

Each leader has to decide what the real tests of adequate hymns are when reduced to a minimum. As a basis for discussion raise questions which deal with how to enlist the entire personality in singing:

Reality—What is true for the singers according to their age, experience, desire, capacity? (Not what is pretty, sweet, or pious.)
Heart—What appeals to their genuine feelings—gladness, amazement, wistfulness, enthusiasm? (Not "goody, goody," or merely sentimental.)

[1] George Herbert, from "A True Hymn."

67

Mind—What furnishes substance to mold into worthy concepts of One whose thoughts are higher than our thoughts? (Not conventional phrases to be mouthed only, but convictions that cost when lived up to.)

Soul—What develops individuality, independence, an inner self, Christian integrity? (Not a rubber stamp or a surface religion.)

Strength—What provides power to give oneself to work with and for others in the Christian cause? (Not content with saying but putting purpose into action.)

Our taste, judgment, and situation will affect our choices, so that the words and music selected will vary widely. Naturally that is the way it should be. The process we go through to reach conclusions, however, is much the same for all. That makes it profitable for the group to talk over how we go about it, so long as none of us leaves the impression that he has arrived at the only right choices. For practice indicate what you would approve for certain age levels in order to fulfill a major requirement for each stage. The minister, music director, church school superintendent, and teachers, who map out month to month demands for songs and hymns in the program, will do well to get together first to agree on the values they are seeking. For a synopsis to serve as suggestion, rather than a chart, four areas referred to above are staked out with three selections set down in each for as many age levels.

Desirable Emotional Content

1. For primary and junior years: "The Year's at the Spring," Robert Browning; tune: "English Christmas Carol." [2]

Enjoyment of sights and sounds outdoors; inner sense of security and rightness in a world ruled by God, in and despite outward circumstances. Read the whole poem "Pippa Passes," by Robert Browning, before telling the story of Pippa, a child singing. She has only one day off from her work in a silk mill during the entire year.

Put yourself in Pippa's shoes. Imagine what she is doing and thinking.

What does Pippa see and sing about?

What is there which she cannot see that she puts into her song?

How are the two connected?

Sing, as Pippa did, the tune without being accompanied, then hear how much the piano can add to a second singing of the song.

[2] For another, two-part, setting see Thomas, *The Whole World Singing*, p. 72.

THE YEAR'S AT THE SPRING

Robert Browning, 1841   From Sandys' Christmas Carols, 1833

The year's at the spring, And day's at the morn; Morn-ing's at

sev - en; The hill - side's dew - pearled; The lark's on the wing; The

snail's on the thorn: God's in his heav - en, All's right with the world!

Music copyright 1935 by Edith Lovell Thomas. *Singing Worship,* No. 71.

2. For teen-agers: "All Creatures of Our God and King," St. Francis, translated by W. H. Draper; tune: "Lasst uns erfreuen," German melody.[3]

Love of God, Giver of life in the universe, our home; taking satisfaction in the good things that belong to all but which none can buy.

Precede singing with a thumbnail sketch of St. Francis, "Troubadour of God," [4] who put into this only hymn he ever wrote the atoneness of all life with the Creator when seen in true perspective.

Teen-agers easily identify themselves with all creatures, readily feeling "reverence for life" as great souls like Albert Schweitzer do. This is a hymn with which to crystallize such emotional attitudes.

3. For young people: "Let All the World in Every Corner Sing,"

[3] *Singing Worship* (Abingdon-Cokesbury Press), *Hymns for Junior Worship* (Westminster Press).

[4] See Sophie Jewett, *God's Troubadour* (Thomas Y. Crowell Co.).

George Herbert; tunes: "High Road," Martin Shaw, or "Universal Praise," W. G. Whinfield (Protestant Episcopal *Hymnal*), or "All the World," John Porter (*The Methodist Hymnal*).

A glowing personal experience of world-wide fellowship found by opening the heart in singing to the Lord of all people.

The English author was devoted to a poor country church of which he was the rector. His love of music shines through the lines. The poem is found in *The Temple: or Sacred Poems and Private Ejaculations,* entrusted to a friend to publish after Herbert's death "if he can think it may turn to the advantage of any dejected soul."

Expression of Basically Christian Thoughts

1. For primary and junior ages: "Far Away in Old Judea," Walter J. Mathams; tune: "Judea," Carey Bonner (*Singing Worship, The Whole World Singing*).

God is shown to be like Jesus, companion of children, as of adults, in creative, adventurous experience.

To make lifelike use with a picture having the appeal of Tom Curr's "Follow Me." In this interpretation children of several nationalities are starting off for a walk with Jesus. A path to shining hills beckons. Jesus, with a smiling face, appears to be an irresistible guide to the eager group of boys and girls. Conversation touching what probably was seen and learned from Jesus during the walk, bringing in what picture and poem hint, can lead naturally into "stories Jesus told them of our Father's thoughtful care." How this care is exercised can be discussed so that the leader learns the thoughts it arouses in the children's minds.

2. For teen-agers: "My Master Was a Worker," William George Tarrant; tune: "Meirionydd," William Lloyd (*The Beacon Song and Service Book*). Different settings in other hymnals.

To deepen insight into what it means to be a Christian, that is, to be an apprentice of the Master in spirit, thought, word, and action. Study of this hymn might challenge the group to name boys and girls, men and women, of the present and past who demonstrate Christian character in action.

3. For young people and adults: "O Brother Man, Fold to Thy Heart Thy Brother," John G. Whittier; tune: "Lanherne," Henry Hayman (*New Worship and Song*). Almost every hymnal has a different setting. Finding a fitting one is difficult.

"To worship rightly is to love each other" is a key line to this poem of an American Quaker. It reveals a principle that dominated the author's writing, speaking, and working, primarily in trying to arouse the nation to treat the Negro in a brotherly way and free him from slavery. The influence Whittier exerted on statesmen and on Christian thinking regarding the worth of every human being is beyond reckoning.

The hymns of Whittier, at first poems to be read, not sung, now in almost all hymnals, have brought together diverse denominations and strengthened church unity toward which we slowly move.

That Which Will Develop Whole Persons

1. For primary children: "Thank Thee, God," Frances M. Hill; tune: "Christus, der ist mein Leben," Melchior Vulpius (*The Whole World Singing*).

To help children discover values to live by; cultivate the habit of appreciating their Source; taking time to observe attentively, to comment thoughtfully; to express in poetic form what is seen of beauty and goodness, and to pose their questions seeking answers. Lifting to the level of thanks a prayer song of this quality, dealing with common impressions made upon the senses, the realm of the invisible is reached in the final stanza:

> We thank thee, God,
> For thoughts of men,
> And deeds of worth;
> For those whose lives and love reveal
> Thy will on earth.[5]

This is not the end of the journey. It is but a pause for breath before pushing on to further valuings that the group is searching to put into singing words.

2. For teen-agers and young people: "He Who Would Valiant Be," John Bunyan; tune: "St. Dunstan's," Winfred Douglas (Protestant Episcopal *Hymnal* and *New Hymnal for American Youth*).

"I'll not fear what men may say," moral stamina born of purpose and persistence in face of discouragement, difficulty, and opposition. John Bunyan is in jail for his faith. Instead of yielding to despair he writes his religious autobiography, *Pilgrim's Progress,* of which this hymn is a part. Is the cost of being a Christian today less than it was then? Ask the teen-agers and the young people to itemize the costs and to reckon whether it is worth taking on the risks.

[5] Used by permission of the author, Frances M. Hill.

3. For adults: "Ye Servants of God, Your Master Proclaim," Charles Wesley; tune: "Hanover," William Croft (*The Methodist Hymnal*).

Not in the isolation of a prison but composed "to be sung in a tumult" was this proclamation. Plenty of tumult there was amid which Charles Wesley, writer of hymns, and John Wesley, preaching the gospel, emancipated a vast number of people from bondage to weakness and fear. Standing firm before the violence of a mob that would silence and destroy the messenger of God they sang lines from this hymn, now omitted from our hymnals:

> Their fury shall never our steadfastness shock;
> The weakest believer is built on a Rock.

That was not rhetoric. That was a historic fact which remade the religious life of England through the zeal and integrity of the people who became known as "Methodists."

An Urge to Reach Out

1. For kindergarten and primary children: "Food for All" (table grace), Edith Lovell Thomas; tune by Franz Schubert (*Sing, Children, Sing*).

To learn how to connect praying and sharing; using the plural first personal pronoun in place of the singular—"*Our* Father," "Give *us*," to become outgoing rather than ingrowing.

Singing this song has to be merged with giving food, money, self in a spirit of concern where the boys and girls can help wtih humility. Communication in person or by letter carried on between the two parties makes each one both giver and receiver and thus doubly blessed.

2. For young people: "Awake, Awake to Love and Work," Geoffrey A. Studdert-Kennedy; tune: "Sheltered Dale," German melody (*The Methodist Hymnal*).

"Thy soul ablaze," "To spend thyself," "To serve right gloriously" are words from the hymn, characteristic of the author who was an English chaplain in the first World War. He made himself "a staunch friend and a strong helper" wherever he went.

3. For adults: "Heralds of Christ," Laura S. Copenhaver; tune: "Pro Patria," Horatio W. Parker (*Church School Hymnal for Youth*).

The Good News is to be told with daring and imagination. This dramatic map of missions is an invitation to young people and adults to make use of modern resources in broadcasting, engineering, medicine, music, agriculture, nursing, all for the glory of God and the spreading of the gospel to every part of the world. Creating peace and good will to dispel war and suspicion is the enterprise summoning all Christians, an adventure above all others most compelling.

Many other aspects of hymn singing should come under scrutiny, and numerous approaches studied by which the most rewarding values can be reached. Some of these come at once to mind—the seasonal, special occasion, that which lends emphasis or interpretation to the curriculum being taught, words improvised for singing to familiar tunes which record a fresh experience, and those that give life to historic persons or events, these are a few of the most obvious.

In almost all the illustrations noted, whether the classification given was musical or hymnic, the choice has been made with tune and text regarded as a unit, each complementing the other and neither complete without the other. In introducing a new hymn the better policy is to lay emphasis upon either the words or the music rather than upon both at the same time. A second time, if advisable, the other element is stressed and its contribution given attention.

Not all sources of the songs and hymns are indicated. Fuller notations are found in "Music Sources," pages 155-160. Typical and representative items are featured among the illustrations, and one or two books in which to look for them are named. Most of the hymns are found in several books, often with different tunes.

All good workmen draw up plans embodying their sorted out purposes. These have to be adapted to change in conditions and to satisfy the claims of the people to be served. Being sensitive to what changes are called for will lead one to improve rather than scrap the original plans. Influencing of human beings through music is too delicate an operation to leave to chance.

Worship combines all the arts and is itself the greatest of all arts. Study of its contents and learning the science of utilizing them wisely make leaders try to keep in contact with informed sources.

Every church library should be equipped to give aid to the leaders through such indispensable books as these have proved to be:
1. Hymnal Manuals (to give only a few) :

These contain comments on the words and music of every hymn and tune in the given hymnal.

Handbook to the Hymnal: William Chalmers Covert, Calvin W. Laufer, Presbyterian Board of Christian Education, 1935.

Handbook to the Lutheran Hymnal: W. G. Polack, Concordia Publishing House, 1942.

Hymnal 1940 Companion, The: Joint commission on the revision of the hymnal of the Protestant Episcopal Church in the U.S.A., 1949.

Songs of Praise Discussed, Handbook to the best-known hymns and to others recently introduced, compiled by Pearcy Dearmer, with notes on the music by Archibald Jacob, Oxford University Press, 1933.

Our Hymnody: Robert G. McCutchan, Handbook to *The Methodist Hymnal,* Abingdon-Cokesbury Press, 1937.

2. Selected Hymns and Tunes:
Backgrounds and suggestions of ways to use hymns in worship.
Lyric Religion: H. Augustine Smith, Fleming H. Revell Co., 1931.

3. Hymnody (dealing with the words only) :
Gospel in Hymns, The: Albert E. Bailey, Charles Scribner's Sons, 1950.

Hymns in the Lives of Men: Robert G. McCutchan, Abingdon-Cokesbury Press, 1945.

Three Centuries of American Hymnody: Henry Wilder Foote, Harvard University Press, 1940.

4. Church Music:
Church Music in History and Practice: Winfred Douglas, Charles Scribner's Sons, 1937.

Music in the History of the Western Church: Edward Dickinson, Charles Scribner's Sons, 1927.

CHOOSE AND CONDUCT SINGING OF SONGS AND HYMNS

1. Appoint three leaders: (1) for children's group—kindergarten and/or primary age; (2) for juniors and/or teen-agers; (3) for young people and/or adults.

2. Each leader comes prepared to teach one of the hymns here printed to interest, suit the capacity, and aim toward a specific religious value consistent with the age level. If a small group of juniors or teen-agers is available to come in for a brief period to be taught a hymn, much can be learned by both the instructors and the singers. Planning how to teach a song or hymn is a very different

process from actually practicing it with a singing group for whom it has been selected.

3. Members of the class may give advance suggestions to the leaders as to how to approach the respective ages they work with and know best. Perhaps the leaders might demonstrate, with the class helping, how each number would be differently introduced to a younger and an older group.

"Plum Blossoms"

1. Learned by kindergarten children:

Play method: hearing the story; being the plum, or any other more familiar tree, in center of the circle—one or more children with outstretched arms for branches and finger tips opening out from buds into blossoms; rest of the circle stepping on tiptoe toward tree to the seven-note phrase, in rhythm, resting a beat, then moving seven steps backward on the second phrase, pausing, and repeating moving toward and away from the tree; standing still on fifth and sixth lines to point out and marvel at the countless number of blossoms discovered on the tree. The leader sings the story, pianist accompanying; children play the scene, and join in singing as they fall under the spell of the song.

Religious values: becoming sensitive to beauty that is free for the taking; breathless sense of wonder at the change from seeming death to life as conveyed by Japanese art in the fewest words and childlike music; pausing in the presence of mystery; expressing delight in the miracle that "hath made everything beautiful in its time." [6]

2. As primary children might appropriate the song:

Seeing, touching, observing a branch of plum blossoms, or visiting the tree: discovering form, arrangement of buds, blossoms, leaves, time required for developing ideas; adding a second stanza into which would go findings, questions, exclamations. Lacking the actual fruit tree and its flowers, supply the loveliest pictures of them to be had, particularly Japanese prints when obtainable. Some of the reverence which Japanese people feel for growing things may be communicated to the children through this medium. Singing a song of school children from the opposite side of the world more sympathetically follows some such line of doing and thinking.

Same values sought as with the kindergarten age, to be realized in a more mature way.

[6] Ecclesiastes 3:11 A.S.V.

PLUM BLOSSOMS

Translated by Sarah C. Kramer
From the Japanese
Delicately

Sung in Japanese Kindergartens
Harmony added

Sweet plum blos-soms, fine and white, Did you o - pen in the night?

Yes - ter - day the tree was bare, Now it's cov-ered eve - ry-where!

One and two and three and four! I can-not count how ma - ny more!

Used by permission of the translator, Miss Sarah C. Kramer. The plum is said to be the first tree to blossom in every Japanese schoolyard.

"Awake, Awake to Love and Work"

1. Teaching juniors:

Remembering how visual-minded this age is and how strong the combination of eye and ear appeal can be, think of some large color print, for example, Breton's "Song of the Lark." Put this at the center of attention to highlight the joyous privilege of performing work unselfishly. The group reads aloud the whole hymn, or single good readers are asked to read each stanza in turn. "What, if any, things in the picture," you ask, "are mentioned in the hymn?" "What actions are you urged to take?" (Awake, shout, give, etc.) "Why all this activity?" As soon as the restless energies of the boys and girls are harnessed to working on the sense of the words, swiftly channel them into singing the swinging melody without slackening effort. Make the accent strong, stride vigorous, and the pace steady, not fast.

Religious value: to view useful work, well done, as sacred, because it is the chance for partnership with God in giving to others what has been given to us.

AWAKE, AWAKE TO LOVE AND WORK

Geoffrey A. Studdert-Kennedy   German traditional melody

1. A - wake, a - wake to love and work, The lark is in the sky,
2. Come, let thy voice be one with theirs, Shout with their shout of praise;
3. To give and give, and give a - gain, What God hath giv - en thee;

The fields are wet with dia - mond dew, The worlds a - wake to cry
See how the gi - ant sun soars up, Great lord of years and days!
To spend thy - self nor count the cost, To serve right glo - rious - ly

Their bless-ings on the Lord of Life, As He goes meek-ly by.
So let the love of Je - sus come And set thy soul a - blaze:
The God who gave all worlds that are, And all that are to be.   A-MEN.

G. A. Studdert-Kennedy, *The Unutterable Beauty* (Harper & Bros., New York; Hodder & Stoughton, Ltd., London). Used by permission.

2. How can teen-agers get more from this hymn than juniors?

Though the procedure of learning may be similar for both levels, the insights of younger and older groups will be quite different, as will also their application to exactly what service each is in duty bound to render. On the upper level there would be greater capacity to analyze what gifts individually and collectively are possessed to be invested and how. Real answers to this searching question should be volunteered. The urgency of an all-out campaign should be felt and responded to in unison, or two-part singing.

"Heralds of Christ Who Bear the King's Commands" [7]

1. For young people:

Of various, perhaps equally effective, means of opening up this hymn the biographical one has good possibilities for young people, passing through the period of decision on vocations to which to dedicate their lives. Citations may be read of those who have made the most difference to the world because of bearing "immortal tidings," building highways, through deserts and jungles, to prepare the way of peace across the world. This can be done preliminary to, or in connection with, the perusal of these dramatic words. Awed by what is owed for precious things received, the consecration of self to payment of the debt may become a momentous act, in silent reading of the third stanza, while the music is played softly. It may be that the prayer, read aloud slowly in unison, without accompaniment, would complete the experience with more intensity.

2. For adults:

This hymn could be examined to see if it would serve as a commissioning ritual for teachers in the church school, conducted in a church service, as they take up their work in the fall. Could there grow out of it a statement, jointly prepared, regarding what commands of the King they are to bear to their pupils, and what is the exact nature of the news they bring? Could a litany be written to express more fully what the group would seek for together to enlarge their faith and unite their labors, to make concrete the petition found in the final stanza?

For this class it might become a hymn to strengthen the purpose and practice of the fellowship of musical ministry. Mrs. Copenhaver, the author, tells of the motivation which prompted the making of this hymn in *Our Hymnody* by Robert G. McCutchan, pages 466-67.

[7] Music in Chapter IV, p. 66.

NURSERY AND KINDERGARTEN CLASSES

To see a World in a grain of sand,
And a Heaven in a wild flower,
Hold Infinity in the palm of your hand,
And Eternity in an hour.[1]

Beginnings in Nursery Class

"SHOULD children in the nursery class of the church ever be allowed to sing 'Old Macdonald Had a Farm'?" asked a person anxious to have every item in the program plainly religious. Passing the nursery class door she had heard more than once bits of this old favorite drifting into the hall, and she was troubled.

"I cannot say," replied the teacher addressed, "until I know what the children do with it and what their teacher makes out of it." This was going on in her group: Bobby came to the nursery class for the first time that very morning. Not knowing the children or the teacher he was frightened and tearful. Keeping aloof he made no effort to take part in what was happening. Only when a record was being played did he feel a trifle more at ease. Noticing him as he sat apart, the teacher asked, "Do you know a song, Bobby?"

"Yes, I do."

"Will you sing it?"

"Old Macdonald" was the response, sung so well that respect was won from the children, and a sense of belonging crept into Bobby. By way of a tune he knew Bobby entered the new situation, closed to him before he was given a chance to sing. The teacher opened this door into a larger room, full of opportunity to live religiously. The Christian principle that it is more satisfying to give than to receive was at work. Giving and receiving are complementary, and both are touched with joy.[2]

[1] William Blake, "Auguries of Innocence."
[2] From an experience described by Edith E. Pollard, Director of the Church Nursery School, Christ Church Methodist, New York, New York.

79

In this initial contact with the nursery class in the church the boy experienced a real value before he was expected to put it into words. To try to sing a religious thought before it is rooted in experience is to look for a fruit that has dropped from the blue without benefit of cultivation.

The Blake poem heading this chapter glimpses the insights of an adult who understands the mind and heart of a child. To look with him at a grain of sand or a flower, to hold mystery in the hand and to be really alive is to be a true companion to young children. By this kind of approach the child and one who would guide him can both be truly religious.

We ask "why" when we seek to know the cause and effect, means and end, which control the teaching procedure. The material is secondary, the prime consideration being what goes on in the inner life of the one who is learning. The child learns when he is taught according to his need and his readiness to be taught. His condition and attitudes must be recognized at the outset before they can be served aright. His growth as a Christian person is stimulated or stunted to the degree that his helper understands, or disregards, this unfailing law of spiritual nurture.

There is no list of songs guaranteed to hasten this miracle of growth though there are many songs calculated to create a favorable soil for its upspringing. Songs are one fruitful means supplied when the children appear ready for food for the spirit that is one of music's unique gifts.

There may be little singing by the children at this earliest period, but constant planting and cultivation will produce the song in due season. Rhythmic motives accompanying their play, imitation of sound patterns to which attention is called, and response often repeated to musical signals when used in place of words—all accustom the children to listening habits. Encouraging the boys and girls to match tones when their names are called on a high, low, or middle pitch is an easy game that is fun and good ear training. See musical conversation hints in chapter III, "Music Made at Home," for experiments to try.

The wide-awake teacher observes the urge to make noise and tries to convert it from mere noise into pleasing sound or purposeful action. Here is a growing edge to be watched and tended.

Young ears pick up sounds quickly, and their owners react promptly in kind. "There's music in the air" of the nursery class where real growing is taking place. The snatch of a hymn tune sung or hummed by the teacher moving about the room. The air for "This is my Father's World" is infectious in its influence. A happy moment is prolonged by the pianist who spontaneously plays a short theme having the gaiety of Schubert's "Moment Musical," Opus 94, No. 3. The muted tones of the grownup's voice, as she talks with the children, are taken up by them unconsciously. These media definitely color the environment of children with agreeable sensations and arouse curiosity. The youngsters prick up their ears to catch new meanings. In countless connections God allows us to mediate his love to them through the attitudes they absorb from us who associate with them. How could they become more directly "rooted and grounded in love"?

Besides rousing the children to hear and give back a pattern, the "Who-ee" song[3] is one that gets them to use their eyes also. "Listen" and "look" are common words in their vocabulary. Everywhere are value experiences that await ears which are alert and that attract wide-open eyes. Pictures in the sky and the music of nature's sounds are daily fare for all who will partake. Let the wonder and beauty that arrest the senses sink into the child's imagination and emotion, and behold it remade by him into the joys of poetry and music. Encourage it; do not interrrupt the flow of it. Allow him to form his own conclusions rather than expect him to repeat your own statements. Sing back to him a poetic remark he makes. Pick up a tune he hums as he is playing, and let the piano show him how it sounds while he listens. Hum it over until others imitate it. As radio plucks music out of the air, so the teacher, an even more sensitive instrument, captures the unseen and unheard music with meaning for children because she understands their cravings.

· Leave moralizing out of your comments and don't spoil what is complete for the moment in the child's experiencing by sticking in what is foreign to his views.

When the teacher notes signs of musical interest, she speaks to the children on different pitch levels to sharpen tone consciousness, introduce whimsy into what she says, and avoid monotony of too much talking. Look back to Chapter III for illustrations.

From singing-speech it is a short step to two-tone, or wider-range songs, of four-measure length, repeated, or eight measures.

Singing combined with action is easy when the pattern is simple and plain to follow. The children make up their own directions and

[3] Music at end of chapter.

describe what they are doing in musical vocabulary: something like this, bowing from the waist with hands on hips, they sing "Bend low" on a descending interval—G-D below. As they straighten up, G-D above is sung, the down and up movements with their tunes being done over and over, until action and music become one and practically automatic. Any number of inventions of things to do together and ways to sing about them begin in this fashion, and make a lot of fun while the children are learning to co-ordinate use of their muscles and their vocal cords.

It's time for the midmorning snack of fruit juice and crackers. As the group sits at the table, they intone (sing on one pitch), "It's good to eat and drink!" "We like fruit juice. We like crackers." "Thank you, ———"—naming the one who put the snack on the table. "Thank you, God," is said as soon as the children understand something of the relationship between work and enjoying what God gives. Using the word "God" without knowing for what or whom it stands is as futile as inserting the name of a person who is an utter stranger to the child. Indeed it is worse than futile for it prevents him from contact with the Reality which is God that he would make if blundering adults did not get in his way.

The purpose of saying grace is to encourage the attitude of gratitude until it becomes habitual so that, as Charles Lamb says, each one is "disposed to say grace upon twenty other occasions in the course of the day besides (my) dinner." [4]

A good record player and a few choice records to play for and by themselves is desirable for this young group, and they are full of possibilities at each successive stage of growing. To hear a lovely strain of music when coming into the room, a soothing selection at rest time, and to react appropriately to the voice of music and its moods are opportunities that rightfully belong to a church nursery class.

Mrs. Ruth Howard Gray, an experienced teacher, is quoted to show reasons for having records and toy instruments for equipment:

In our nursery and kindergarten groups we use a record-player quite a bit. The children enjoy rhythmic activity in accompaniment to the music . . . some nursery rhymes, folk song type, game songs from our church school literature and music without words, which may at times be classical and at others not. Records

[4] *Essays of Elia.*

82

which the children enjoy most of all are "Rainbow Rhythms."[5] Miss Emerson had the children act or make rhythms such as an elephant walking and the like. Then she composed the music in accord with the children's activity. The three-year-old children especially enjoy these.

Most of this activity takes place in the Sunday morning session and in the vacation church school.

We use triangles and simple home-made instruments, rhythm sticks, blocks, tambourines, sleigh bells, and drums. Because of the enjoyment on the part of the children and also because of the emotional results—especially on the restless and unco-operative—we are planning more and more to incorporate music in our program.[6]

Music lends charm to what is done, not as a separate element, but as an integral part of the entire experience of the nursery class day. We discover how it connects each with the others and speaks to individuals with many voices. Count on the sensitiveness of children wherever music and motion are present, for they are only waiting for help to release the songs inside them. How closely music and life are related! All have the power to fulfill themselves as children of God every time they sing for joy in harmony with all creation.

> There is music in the swaying of the trees,
> There is music in the dancing of the leaves.
> Ah, all the world has music in it,
> But there are very few to sing it.[7]

Seen and Heard in Kindergarten

Beethoven confided in a friend the purpose of one of his sacred choral compositions: "It was my chief aim to awaken and to render lasting religious feeling in the singers as in the listeners." Are these not outcomes which the Christian teacher desires for kindergarten children? Bringing pleasure is certainly one of the first rewards music confers, but a test of its abiding value is the quality of feeling it evokes when heart and mind are awakened by its call.

Visit a kindergarten where this aim is being pursued. The children are strangely silent when there is a chance to sing. The teacher

[5] Recordings for children with vocal introductions, composed, arranged, and recorded by Nora Belle Emerson (3 records, 18 rhythms), Box 608, Emory University, Georgia.

[6] Mrs. Ruth Howard Gray, Director of Children's Work, Glenn Memorial Church, Emory University Campus, Atlanta, Georgia.

[7] Harriet Cannon (eight years old) in Mabel Mountsier, *Singing Youth* (Harper & Bros.). Used by permission of Mabel Mountsier.

is troubled about why the musical response is so slight. What is the cause? A few younger ones, unused to the setting, are shy; the song attempted is unknown to several; the transition from another activity to singing is too abrupt to arouse interest; the adult carries the tune along without allowing the children to sing it alone, or with light support from the piano. Are the children free to speak and sing their thoughts? Did the leader start at the live point where the children were or at a place that she, as an adult, thought would be *good* for them"? The conclusion was that the near, concrete thing that concerned the individuals was sacrificed for the remote, abstract idea beyond or alien to the young mind's grasp.

The song material vitally related to their feelings, grasp, and ability the children will sing, however imperfect the musical result may be.

The next Sunday there is a different approach. The teacher sings a greeting which has drawn the boys and girls together before and is one they like to sing:

> Every morning seems to say,
> "There's something happy on the way,
> And God sends love to you!" [8]

Conversation links thoughts to "something happy" which occurs to them as together they speak of what this very morning brings. Eyes are closed, quiet reigns, hands are raised as glad things come to mind and are rapidly named. Richard speaks. His face is the picture of contentment. His hands, moving in curved lines, suggest the scene shifting from day to night and back again in perfect rhythm. Dreamily his words come:

> The sun goes down
> And the dark comes.
>
> Then the stars come out.
>
> Boats must put their lights on,
> And the docks have lights too.
>
> When the sunshine comes again
> It is another day.

[8] Henry van Dyke, "Something Happy" (Charles Scribner's Sons). Used by permission. Set to music in Edith Lovell Thomas, *Martin and Judy Songs* (The Beacon Press).

Others reflect Richard's satisfaction. More remarks are made in the same vein. Jack, impatiently waiting his turn, breaks in with, "I have a little song which is a lively one, so people like to hear it." By request comes a merry air improvised, carrying the words:

> The little Jesus came down the street.
> Tra, la, tra, la, tra, la!

The gay tune holds the attention of all. Delight, melody, and rhythmic pattern brightly blend to relax and unite the circle more closely. The children make real for themselves their togetherness as glad thoughts are shared. The leader is being taught the way into the children's world and there finds the essence of song.

We do not have to put in the name of God to make sure that a song is religious. Indeed, insincere use of the word becomes only a thoughtless, irreverent habit when it precedes, rather than follows, experience which gives it meaning. The child must be mature enough to form his own ideas instead of repeating adult phraseology glibly. Seeing and hearing ways through which God comes to us, enjoying and expressing the thoughts this contact awakens—these are true foundations upon which worship is built. As Jean Ingelow asserts, "Joy is the grace we say to God." [9] More reticence becomes the teacher who would follow the children's lead in getting at what is true for them instead of insisting that they adopt her adult vocabulary.

A few weeks before Easter the marvel of a tiny seed being transformed into a flower is explored in the Kindergarten. A bowl, bag of earth, and packet of assorted seeds are worked with preliminary to singing a story about growing. The bowl and bag of earth are put in the center of the circle. With hands behind back the teacher challenges, "Guess what is in my hand!" A few guesses and the envelope of seeds is shown having bright-colored blossoms pictured on the outside. They are called by name, as far as information lasts. The group talks over what must be done if the black specks ever turn into flowers. Each child drops a pinch of seeds into the wee garden, covering them with a sprinkling of soil. The stillness that prevails is a prelude for singing the song which picks up the action and repeats it rhythmically in "Look! look! our seeds we're planting!" [10] Since the tune moves up and down scalewise, with only one wider

[9] "Dominion."
[10] See music section at end of chapter.

interval, the children get it quickly after one hearing. The wonder in the question, "Will they grow?" the mystery of sun and rain blessing our work, seeds growing silently from out of sight into small green tips, then upstanding plants are all in the song. What a world of beauty the group enters drawn by music that is linked with sight, word, and action!

A Bible story is made to serve worship when the boys and girls sit before a blue and ivory print of "Jesus and the Children" a Czech girl artist [11] has painted. Children, older and younger, in the picture show deferential attitudes toward the warm personality of Jesus, who sits among them. His interest in each of those who have come to see him is made to appear in a way none can miss. The story is made into verse and set to a Chinese children's tune[12] which continues the theme and brings it into relationship with what is happening in the group's local church calendar.

Once a year this kindergarten with the rest of the church school takes part in a sanctuary service. The baptism of children is one of its traditions. Because of their love of babies and their knowing the story of Jesus welcoming children, the kindergarten helps in the baptism ritual. The church is for them the home of God's family. Contact has been had with the minister of music, who has played the organ for them. They have gone into the sanctuary to see what it holds and what it is for and have sung to organ accompaniment. The minister calls on them and talks with them in a way they understand. Now it is their chance to sing as a part of the big family gathering at the altar where children are brought by parents to be baptized. The song "Children, Come," written for them for this event, now performs its special function. They linger after the song ends, a "cloud of witnesses" around the minister, who takes the babies in his arms. For once, without craning of necks they can follow the rite which absorbs their interest. The background of their earnest faces vivifies the scene for parents and congregation. Their presence dramatizes the fact that they, too, belong to the church family.

The singers express clearly what they have to say. They measure up to their responsibility in a manner that makes them grow.

Another growing edge, too neglected, is evident in this conversation which was converted into a song. The skillful teacher is one of those who love to help children in "Creating Their Own Songs."

[11] Bella Vichon. Artext Prints, Inc., Westport, Connecticut.
[12] Song, "Children, Come!" See end of chapter.

During the conversation period when the children were talking about the New Year, Jan said, "A noise woke me up. My mother told me that a New Year had come. Then on New Year's Day all said, 'Happy New Year' to each other. It was fun." Peter told about the new horn his daddy had bought for him to blow. Jack told about his whistle. After much conversation the teacher asked the children if they would like to make up a song of their own about the New Year. "I can make up a song," said Betty as she began to sing:

The lit - tle new
year is com - ing in.

The children liked Betty's song but Jimmy thought it should say, "Happy New Year to All" at the end. The teacher went to the piano, played the melody and sang the song including the phrase which Jimmy wanted. "That is a *good* song," said Gladys. "Let's sing it that way." At the teacher's suggestion the children decided to sing the phrase, "The little new year is coming in," twice. Then the children began to march around the room singing the new song.

The lit-tle new year is
com - ing in; The lit-tle new
year is com - ing in.
Hap-py New Year, Hap-py New
Year, Hap-py New Year to all. [13]

Songs created by children may be pathways to worship.

A teacher was guiding a small group of four-year-olds in a laboratory school class using the manual *Let's Go Out-of-Doors* by Jennie Lou Milton. During several rainy days the children had planted seeds and watered them but could

[13] Rosemary K. Roorbach in *Child Guidance in Christian Living.* Copyright 1946 by Stone & Pierce. Used by permission.

have no outdoor experiences. On the first sunny day the teacher took them out on a "looking trip."

They paused under a tree on a hill and looked up at the sky, noticing the fleecy, moving clouds. They sang together:

> For trees that stretch out wide and tall,
> For white clouds floating over all,
> Thank you, loving Father.[14]

The teacher, quickly improvising another stanza, sang:

> For birds that fly up so high,
> For soft, white clouds and blue, blue sky,
> Thank you, God, our Father.

The children joined her in singing the "thank you" refrain. As they walked down the hill, a boy began to chant:

> Thank you, God,
> Thank you, God,
> Thank you for the trees.

> Thank you, God,
> Thank you, God,
> Thank you for the sky.

The teacher knelt beside the child and sang the chant with him. Some of the other children paused and gathered around, singing with them. For a moment there was real worship as the teacher and the children thanked God together in the words of a child's own song.

On another walk, after a rainy day, they paused to watch the custodian transplanting plants. This they understood, for they had had experiences getting their fingers in dirt as they had planted growing things in flower pots. A child began to chant:

> He can help God,
> He can help God,
> He can help God,

"To make the flowers grow," added the teacher. Then the teacher sang:

> I can help God,
> I can help God,
> I can help God
> To make the flowers grow.

---

[14] Copyright 1935 by Jennie Lou Milton.

The children sang the words with her. Again, for a brief moment, there was a mood of worship in the group.[15]

Find out in every way you can how the songs to which a child is exposed are being absorbed by him—what he does with them outside the class as well as how he responds to their stimulus during the program. One teacher attempts to make the visual images in the song's words clear to the boys and girls by putting the verses into large individual scrapbooks, for which the children make pictures or paste in illustrations cut from magazines.

In your record where you treasure incidents, and what the children say, do you have signs that music makes a difference to them?

One mother[16] takes comfort in the use her son found for one of his songs telling "Our daughter had just returned home following a tonsillectomy. Her brother, who was three, was delighted to see her and could not let her out of his sight. After Mary was settled in bed, Mickey carried a little chair close to her, sat down, beamed, and then burst into a song he had first learned in the church nursery class:

> When I'm very happy
> This is what I sing,
> "Thank you, God, I thank you
> Just for everything." [17]

The belief of Jesus in the innate spiritual gifts of childhood grips us anew with each experiment in putting them to use. Music well employed calls these forth and renders service for which we give thanks. In childlike trust in their ability we pray to be changed into those whose eyes are on the unseen, allowing our young charges full scope to sing that which is close to their hearts.

Some points to check in judging the fitness of songs for the kindergarten period:

Short and simple tunes—more of four lines than longer; more stepwise, than wider intervals; more straight quarter, eighth, and half notes than dotted notes.

Words easy to say and understand—more one and two syllable words than longer; more familiar vocabulary than new; more con-

[15] Mrs. Joseph G. Bryan, Kansas City, Missouri. Contributed by Nelle Gilmore, Minister of Music and Education, Old First Presbyterian Church, San Francisco, California.

[16] Mrs. Fred V. McDonnell, Carlisle, Pennsylvania.

[17] Copyright 1933 by Mary Edna Lloyd.

crete than general ideas, attached to a child's everyday living, instead of doctrinal ideas or moralizing in adult language.

Natural feeling tone—spontaneous gladness, appreciation, hushed attitude, eagerness for a story, wanting to *do* something, like dramatic or rhythmic play.

Giving wings to imagination—including humor, looking through brightly colored glasses to find new friends and go places, missing no pleasures.

Sense of security—need to belong to family, church, God.

Right relations with people—friendly feeling for, helpful action, thankful spirit.

Love of beautiful things—themes of good music, connected with the church, poetic verse, fine pictures associated with songs.

Questioning, wondering—exploring mystery, reaching out toward God, Source of all life.

PLAY, FEEL, THINK, SING, WITH THE YOUNGEST

" 'Who-ee! Who-ee!' Sings the Wind"

a. On a breezy day listen to the song of the wind. Imitate the sounds.

Teacher: I'll be the wind. You can be the wind, too. Make just the same sounds that I do. (Teacher sings the first "who-ee," and the children do the second one after, or with her, each time. She sings the rest of the story. Perhaps the children will describe with their hands, or entire bodies, where the wind sings.)

Teacher: Sometimes I come very near you and my voice is strong. (Sing the "who-ee's" emphatically.) Sometimes I am far away and you hear me sighing. (Very softly.)

b. On a rainy day listen to what the rain is saying before singing the second stanza. Watch to see from what direction the drops come and how they behave on the windowpanes. Sing the "spatter" fast or slow according to the brisk or gentle movement of the rain. Perhaps the children can set the pace and volume, and the teacher copy them.

An individual or several children may soon be able to do the wind song and others choose to take the rain's part while all the rest sing the story. Lend as much help as needed, but no more, so that the group may have the fun of singing by themselves. Bring in the piano part softly when it will aid rather than hinder group singing. As the children first hear the piano playing the accompaniment, they may want to sway, clap, or dance to the rhythms they feel to be present.

c. Great changes are happening in the sky which are to be looked for and listened to in silence. Then each child gets his turn to tell what he sees and hears.

Teacher:

> Listen! Listen! Look and see!
> What are you hearing?
> What are you seeing?
> Stop now! Listen! Look and tell! [18]

WHO-EE!

Edith Lovell Thomas   German Melody

(Another Child)   (Group)   (All)

2. "Spatter! Spatter!" says the Rain,
   "Spatter! Spatter!" says the Rain,

   Here on this window,
   There on that window.

   (Child)

   "Spatter! Spatter!" says the Rain.

3. Listen! Listen! Look and see!
   Listen! Listen! Look and see!

   Wind has stopped singing,
   Rain has stopped talking.

   Blue sky! Blue sky! Clouds blown away!

Edith Lovell Thomas, *Martin and Judy Songs,* No. 9. Copyright 1948 The Beacon Press. Used by permission.

[18] Written for this book.

Children say what they have been noticing. The answers may fit into the meter of the song, or the words of the third stanza may tell the tale, so that the children can join with the leader, accompanied by piano, in singing the blue sky chapter from beginning to end.

Playing with above stanzas will take three experiments, probably tried on as many days.

Aim: to practice hearing and seeing observantly as a prelude to singing with the whole self. This is the beginning of making music accurately and expressing through it what is true and beautiful.

"Look! Look! Our Seeds We're Planting"

On pages 85-86 is given an account of one kindergarten acting out the cycle of growth of seeds, sprouting from friendly soil to upstanding plants. The wonder of this slow change and its dependence upon the co-operation of planter with soil, sun, and rain takes time to drink in. Suppose we let music play its part in preparing us for this miracle.

a. Before the pianist plays the music of the song, the teacher says if the day is bright, "You are going to hear for just a moment sunshiny music. See if your eyes can find something that sunlight is resting on." (Music played with good volume in quick tempo.) Children mention what the light does for the things it touches.

If it is rainy weather, the game is to think about or discover how the rain affects what it touches outdoors, during the playing of the song slowly and softly. The need growing things have for both sun and rain is stressed.

b. The pianist, or leader, with accompaniment, sings the second stanza at a medium pace with the sun lines done brightly and the rain part lightly.

c. Now that the children have heard the melody three times, with one saying of the words they should be able to carry the tune of the second stanza with or without help.

d. The teacher suggests that the weather seems to be all right for planting some seeds (name what). Then follows the actual doing of the planting act and the singing of the first stanza.

Singing and doing are interspersed, the work done, and the song learned alternately.

e. The third stanza, saved until the new growth appears, is sung as there is excitement over developments to be made vocal. Or it may be more satisfying to use the whole song in the 2-1-3 order of stanzas (or 1-2-3) to keep the entire cycle of growth in mind.

Aim: to feel the interrelationship of ourselves with all life and our dependence, with all growing things, upon sun and rain and work for our very life.

LOOK!

Anonymous   Norwegian

1. Look!__ look! our seeds we're plant-ing In __ a __ row.
Soft-ly, soft-ly, cov-er them o - ver. Will they__ grow?

2. Look! Look! the sun is shining   3. Look! Look! the plants are growing.
   Warm and bright.   First they're small.
   Look! Look! the rain is falling   Up! Up! see them standing
   Soft and light.   Straight and tall.

Edith Lovell Thomas, *Martin and Judy Songs* (The Beacon Press), No. 21. Used by permission.

"Children, Come!"

The feeling of being wanted and having a place where one belongs is of greatest importance to a child's development into a normal personality.

The position of the child in the center of family and religious living was given to him by Jesus, and the main function of the church is to provide a spiritual home for children. How one kindergarten group made this song its part in a church family celebration is related on page 86.

A Chinese children's air is the music to which the story was sung, so that the boys and girls might glimpse something of the size and variety of the Father's household and not make the mistake of thinking that they are his only sons and daughters.

The rhythmic pattern, when it is tapped out, sounds like the patter of feet going toward Jesus, walking, running, hesitating. Tapping one line at a time, let the children try to reproduce it to catch the excitement of the event. The children will sketch in the details of the song story assisted by the Bible passage and the picture interpretation, which will be all the introduction stanzas 1 and 2 require. After merging them with the melody, omitting the harmony at first, they are ready to think of their own church as the place where all people can come and be made to feel at home. The accompaniment, now put in with the singing of the third stanza, emphasizes the impression of togetherness which the words try to convey.

CHILDREN, COME!

Edith Lovell Thomas   Chinese Air

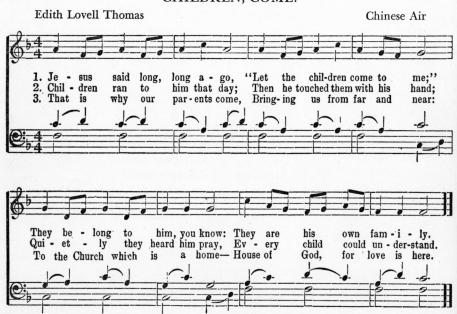

1. Je - sus said long, long a - go, "Let the chil-dren come to me;"
2. Chil - dren ran to him that day; Then he touched them with his hand;
3. That is why our par - ents come, Bring-ing us from far and near:

They be - long to him, you know: They are his own fam - i - ly.
Qui - et - ly they heard him pray, Ev - ery child could un - der-stand.
To the Church which is a home— House of God, for love is here.

Written for this book.

CHAPTER VII

PRIMARY BOYS AND GIRLS

Opening out a way
Whence the imprisoned splendor may escape.[1]

PEACHES are one of the main crops on a large Canadian farm. With what care this fruit is grown, how the entire family and a host of neighbors have to work to cultivate, harvest, and market the produce, is described by a daughter who participates. Duties are divided so that the father and each son specialize in soil chemistry or knowing the best brands of fruit, when to plant, prune, spray, gather, and protect the trees during the hard winter. All the family put together their knowledge, skill, and labor to perfect the culture of the finest peaches. This is a particular, tiring process, long and slow, for there is a wait of several years after planting till the fruit matures, and the life of a bearing peach tree is short.

The story is a sort of parable for us who are intent upon nurturing children in Christian living so that they will grow "straight and strong like saplings." [2] How diligent and persistent we have to be to find out what music supplies to the maturing of tender young lives!

The nursery and kindergarten stages of preparing soil, planting seeds, and sprouting time now passed, what signs of growing do we anticipate and foster during the primary period?

Fuller and More Satisfying Musical Activities

Public school teachers speak of what they have learned in this regard:

Motivation is the most important single factor in learning. Yet our educational institutions tend to stifle, rather than to foster in children strong, vital interests in what we believe is important for them to learn.[3]

[1] Robert Browning.
[2] Psalm 144:12 Moffatt.
[3] Foreword, *Fostering Mental Health in Our Schools,* 1950 Yearbook, Association for Supervision and Curriculum Development, National Education Association.

Every child must have help in growing toward the goal of an emotionally mature adulthood. . . . We are recognizing our responsibility for helping children to learn to feel in certain ways.[4]

In some instances, the teacher's problem is not so much that of utilizing the child's spontaneous interests and motives. It is rather a problem of helping children to *develop* interests and motivations. This is particularly true of those boys and girls who . . . have had meager experience, who have not had opportunity for exploring wide areas of activity.

A woman was speaking recently of her lack of appreciation of music: "I grew up in a family where none of us had any interest in music. I never heard any music at home, and I never cared. But I can remember as if it were yesterday something which happened to me in school. . . . We were supposed to learn to sing, it seems, and I wasn't sure if I wanted to or not. The idea began to appeal to me, though, as the boys and girls around me followed the teacher's lead and began to sing about spring and the sunshine.

"But it didn't turn out so well. The teacher walked up and down the aisles, listening to each of us. As she came near, I decided to sing loud if not well. So I gave it everything I had. When she came to me, she stopped, shuddered, and said,

" 'Ugh! Don't sing—you're spoiling it all.'

"And I didn't sing—not from that time to now."

Suppose we contrast this woman's experience with the experience the children in the following school are having:

A group of elementary school teachers found that the music experiences were limited both in the amount of time devoted to them and to the variety of activities. . . .

In the primary classrooms where only rote-singing had been practiced the program was enriched by introducing a rhythm band. Children and teachers talked about instruments which could be made. . . . They began looking for them to bring from home. Tin tops, horseshoes, nails, coffee cans, combs, wood blocks, bottles, toy drums, and rattles of different kinds were found, and youngsters began trying their skill in constructing instruments which could be used for making music. In time, every youngster had some instrument of his own and the groups began playing together by playing rhythm band arrangements.

Some found it easy to sing while playing. Some developed a real feeling for rhythm. By the end of the year the children were making arrangements of their own. Singing became a major activity. Many singing games, in and out of school, were enjoyed. . . .

The enjoyment of these activities inspired children to put words to familiar tunes, and later to create tunes of their own. The children were given many opportunities to respond to music through creative dancing. . . . Some children

[4] Bernice Neugarten and Nelle Wright in *ibid.*

who showed creative ability in music actually became better adjusted in other work.[5]

Participation is something to obtain in younger children, but primary children can give that and much more. Pure, unforced singing quality, clear speaking, and good teamwork are now expected of them. Vocabulary, interests, and power of expression are broadening; and music is a way of conveying what they want to say which can't be said in any other fashion.

Certain fundamentals of music must be learned to serve the new demands. There is no reason why a child who is finding out how to read a printed page should be kept ignorant of the staff, note values, and how to follow a tune outline. With a little practice, incidental and held to a minimum, this sign language, about which the youngsters are curious, can be handled like a game—how to tell a walking note (quarter) from a running one (eighth), how long to hold a white note, why have bars, when to clap strong beats and weak beats, and what a meter is for. Useful facts of this nature are filtered in while new songs are being acquired, and the monotony of rote teaching is thereby relieved.

Once in a while a tune is introduced by showing how it looks written on a staff in large well-spaced notes, apart from words. It is drawn on a large paper or blackboard where all can see it easily. Attention is called to one or two of the fundamentals referred to above. The pianist plays tune only, to free the ear from other distracting parts, while one child traces its route along the staff with a pointer. Phrase by phrase is played and then is reproduced by the children singing "la, la," with piano silent, to catch how exactly it has been heard; and wrong impressions are corrected before continuing. Combine voices and piano giving out the melody from start to finish, adding for a close the harmony played to accompany the voices.

Employ humming as a way to unite a group before praying, singing the words of a song, or to substitute for a prelude played on the piano. It helps the children pull themselves together to create a legato tone similar to that of an organ and to induce a subdued mood so often needed to dispel confusion from a group activity. From humming "m" shift to "ah" or "oo" to suggest wonder or sighing of the wind. The "Crusader's Hymn," the tune for "Fairest Lord Jesus," is especially good for primary voices. The children can

[5] Caroline Tryon in *ibid.*

learn to hum beautiful church tunes before they are ready for the hymn words belonging to the tunes. These hummed tunes make effective interludes between other worship acts.

After words are printed under the music at a later time the group may draw a decorative border or put in pictures to interpret further what is being sung.

A progressive treatment is carried forward when only one phase of learning is dealt with at a time and briefly. The song sheet is taken away when the children's memory no longer has to be supported by it. Appeals to eye and ear at the same time make for quicker learning than when either one alone is depended on. We are also told that the memory holds longer what is seen than what is heard. Yet how heavily teachers rely on children's hearing to capture and retain what is worth remembering!

The power to concentrate on an activity is growing, but should not be overtaxed. The ability is developing to maintain a back ground of quiet against which music can be heard and made. The orchestral conductor Stokowsky says, "Music is a picture painted on a background of silence." Since radio and television programs now occupy so many waking hours of our children, more help than ever is needed to detect the difference between music not to be missed and the din of sounds one is better off without. So much in religion, as in other aspects of living, depends upon thoughtful listening that church school procedure should give time for practice of the habit. Visual aid of objects, pictures, and printed poetry should be combined with music to fix it in the mind for further reference.

Training in the use of silence is as important as learning to speak and sing together. The two form a normal rhythmic balance. More attention paid to the advice, "Be still and know that I am God," [6] may overcome or lessen the noisy confusion from which today's children suffer so much.

A simple way to encourage a listening habit toward what is worth hearing is to have frequent motives played on piano, organ, or record as a signal to stop whatever is being done, to come together or to begin worship, etc. One of these motives could be an eight-measure theme as notable as the German chorale "Ein' Feste Burg," played two or more successive Sundays for paying attention to arresting sacred music. Only a general label such as "a grand church tune"

[6] Psalm 46:10 A.S.V.

is attached at first, and no hymn words need to be associated with it. Later its name is told with the meaning translated. Humming when it is heard again will stamp it more firmly on the mind. When the music recurs at home, on radio, or in church, and other patterns of beauty become familiar through several hearings, children accumulate musical keepsakes. Cultivating a taste for the best influences choice when a child has a chance to compare the kind he knows with less good music that is showered upon him. People will defend the singing of some hackneyed song by asserting, "But children *love* to sing it." Do they stop to inquire, "Why?" Is it a matter of choosing or because boys and girls are limited perforce to what they know— good, bad, or indifferent—according to what they have heard most often?

What suits their voices, mostly within a medium octave range, (d to d or e to e), uncomplicated rhythm, and with lightly played, simple accompanying harmonies, is studied and tested.

A mother who is concerned about her children having what belongs to them as unfolding persons says,

Music should be a part of the experience of the children themselves, and not superimposed by adults in terms of things that we, and not the children, understand. Our six year old asks us after Sunday school whether a particular song they have been singing is something she can understand, and will I please explain it! I am at a loss to explain to primaries, "Jesus Christ who died for me," or "Heavenly Sunshine, flooding my soul with Glory Divine." I do so wish our three-year-old could be learning something in place of "It's bubbling in my soul, since Jesus made me whole." . . . Wouldn't it be wonderful if all our teachers could and would attend a leadership training course? [7]

More Ability to Direct Themselves Toward Desired Ends

This was shown when second-graders wrote what they do and think about in worship moments:

> Walk slowly,
> Be silent,
> For this is the place
> Where loving and kindness
> Remind us of God.[8]

[7] Mrs. Lewis Whitehead, a minister's wife, LeGrand, California.

[8] Jeanette E. Perkins, *As Children Worship.* Copyright, The Pilgrim Press. Used by permission of the author and publisher.

It was sung to music of their own making[9] by second-grade boys and girls in another church school. One child invented the first melody line, then the others sang it after him. A second line was made up by the next child. These two were sung over by all, and so on, until the tune, altered somewhat, was accepted by the group. They sang it for their primary department, and it was learned and used by the entire group with satisfaction. The singing led into a thoughtful mood that settled into moments of group worship.

Children thrive when they are given time to think and talk together with an adult who opens their eyes to see God at work with people who help him. The group's comments are recorded and matched with music when the impulse comes. Later these thoughts in their musical frame can be passed on to others if it seems good.

Imagination kindled by the poetry and music of suggestive songs carries the children on into a chain of singing answers to questions arising out of what they see and hear, and the meanings that lie behind.

Widening Relations

The primary child moves out into a wide world of people whom he sees or hears stories about—giving help to others, caring for the sick, taking strangers into the home, building schools, and teaching religion. Through personal contact and letters, sharing of gifts and action, he extends himself to find out what it is to "love one another." As a precept the words have little, if any, reality; but as he observes love in action and identifies himself with it, he can truly sing, "The earth is full of the loving kindness of the Lord!" [10] Tracing love and kindness at work back to its Source is a wonderful thing to do. Following their course through the work of hands and feet, hearts, and minds is something to sing about! How impatient Jesus was with saying religious words without doing the right act!

Emotional attitudes aroused by example and put into actual practice, can be strengthened by music. At the core of the Christian religion is that love to God plus love to neighbors that binds all together in helpfulness. "Doing Friendly Things" [11] is a song that goes to the heart of the matter. Primary children sing it with real understanding.

The lovely melody set to these ideas was the tune originally played

[9] Music at end of chapter.
[10] Music at end of chapter.
[11] Music at end of chapter.

on pipes by Italian shepherds as they went about the streets of the town celebrating the birthday of Jesus. Our primary boys and girls link up with the carolers of many lands through the medium of folk tunes and the friendly attitudes engendered by singing one another's songs on holy days that belong to all equally.

To guarantee these values to our primary children co-operative planning must be done, good practice time set aside, and the songs learned must be put to use. They do not happen to come to life if they are not devoted to constructive ends.

The teacher will be supported by the others who are responsible for the educational program—superintendent, minister, music director, pianist—all of whom need to confer as to what should be done and ways and persons to do it.

One minister of Christian education, who also directs the musical program, replies to the question, "How does your church staff co-operate in achieving certain ends?"

Last year our choirs learned to sing the new songs to be introduced in the primary and junior departments so that most of the first stages of learning a new song was accomplished in the choir period during the week. On this project the department superintendent and I would work together.

[At Christmas] the younger children sing carols on the steps of the church as people enter for the vesper service. They have little red hoods and capes and they enjoy sharing in this way.

At Easter we have the little folks go as a group to a few of the sick or shut-ins, who are not too ill, and who enjoy the visit of the children.[12]

The kind of working together that is back of such projects gives the children a chance to relate themselves to older and younger people in the church and parish in mutually helpful ways. A graph which shows at how many points the primary boys and girls make valuable contacts with other individuals and groups in the church should contain many of these lines, increasing in number.

A time for practice on certain Sundays when new material is to be learned is used in place of a worship period occasionally. A fifteen-minute sing as a presession privilege for those who wish to come early, a class meeting in a teacher's home to work up a musical surprise for other classes, a regular weekday hour with the pianist to rehearse numbers to share in Sunday worship, are methods of providing the group with resources.

[12] Grace Mary Williams, First Methodist Church, Oak Park, Illinois.

101

Besides the spontaneous worship expressions, and times devoted to cultivating them, primary musical gifts should be exercised more freely for development and enjoyment. What the children can contribute to church services is essential if they are to feel themselves part of the household of God. It is equally important that their elders recognize the rights and privileges of the younger element who belong even as they do to this household. When Luther, and later Bach, were boys, they with other children were trained to sing all over the town for the birth of a baby, to serenade people to be honored, and to celebrate important civic events. Why should not our children sing to older folk, observe personal anniversaries, and spread good cheer wherever they go, not confining their visits to Christmas caroling?

In view of the primary child's potentials[13] reckon on how to realize them in terms of songs to be learned and put to service; singing them well together; expressing joy, wonder, and other worship moods; making up their own music; using folk songs and churchly hymn tunes; in short, possess to the full their spiritual belongings.

BECOME AS CHILDREN

To feel what it is like to be six, seven, or eight years old ask a person who knows how to lead boys and girls in singing to direct the class in these numbers as he or she would work with a primary group.

Waking Up

Sing something familiar, for example, the French round "Frere Jacques" ("Brother John," music on p. 46). Repeat each line.

> Are you sleeping,
> Brother John?
> Morning bells are ringing:
> Ding, ding, dong!

To alert the class and get them to sing as a unit, warn them you are testing them to see how well they follow a leader. After they hear the round sung once, ask them to sing it without the leader's singing. Then take liberties with the time by beating some lines faster than others, pausing on certain words, etc., after making clear

[13] For further development see the introduction to the author's *Sing, Children, Sing,* "Experiments in Singing with Spirit and Understanding."

what musical signals are to be used. As soon as they become quick and accurate in response to the leader, sing the round in four parts, varying the volume from medium loud to soft according to the leader's guidance. Hold the singers up to the best tonal quality that they can produce in a light head tone, comparable to what you would try to secure from primary children. Caution against allowing any straining of a child's voice, which is so common among teachers who confuse singing loudly with singing well.

At Church: "Before Worship"

To induce a quiet mood.

From the interest and unity engendered by singing the round use a swift, direct method of moving into a mood of quietness and relaxation. This might serve: "Perhaps the music you now hear will make you think of a place to which you often go. Listen to what the music suggests to you!" (Played once softly and slowly.) Accept ideas expressed without comment. "Second-graders made up the tune to sing with these words which they liked." (Quote poem. Leader

BEFORE WORSHIP

Second Grade Children
Riverside Church, New York City

Second Grade Choir
Church in Radburn, New Jersey

Words by Jeanette E. Perkins, *As Children Worship.* Copyright, The Pilgrim Press. Used by permission of the author and publisher.

Musical setting, Edith Lovell Thomas, *The Whole World Singing*, p. 103. Copyright 1950 by Friendship Press, Inc. Used by permission.

sings the song.) "Will you hum with me?" (Piano plays tune only, during humming.) "What two things are you asked to do before worship? Why?" (Repeat words.) With the fewest words needed begin to sing with group words and music, then put them on their own, having piano's help or not. Preserve subdued spirit essential to the inner meaning of the song.

Response or Call to Thinking: "Loving Kindness"

To express appreciation.

Leader: Of what do you suppose the second-graders were thinking when they put into their song, "loving and kindness remind us of God"?

Did you ever *see* love? kindness? How can you tell them? Long ago when people were wondering about this in their book of songs, The Psalms, they wrote "the earth is full of his kindness." [14] Where is it found?

The long-ago people thought he was a kind God because of the earth he made for our home, with the sky above lighted by the sun, moon, and stars, and the great ocean with all its secrets. Perhaps he was most kind of all when he gave to every one of us a mind which we can use for thinking love and kindness toward people who have missed it.

LOVING KINDNESS

Psalm 33:5   Viola W. Franklin

The earth is full of the lov-ing kind-ness of the Lord.

The earth is full of the lov-ing kind-ness of the Lord.

Used by permission of the composer. *Sing, Children, Sing,* No. 13.

[14] Psalm 33:5 Moffatt.

Divide into two groups and let the first half sing after the leader the first phrase, and then the second half reproduce the second phrase. Exchange the phrases between the divisions and end with both groups singing in unison the whole with the playing of the piano.

The song might be sung as the response to a litany beginning with a statement of the children's discoveries, for example. "We have found loving in a mother taking care of her baby," "We have seen kindness when a boy helped a blind man cross the street." Take what is volunteered in pairs and follow with singing the refrain again, stressing the word "full."

"Doing Friendly Things"

To strengthen right relationships.

Leader: Every Christmas the shepherds who cared for their sheep in Italy's hilly country came into the city. They brought shepherd pipes and played tunes in church and up and down the street. When people heard the music of the pipes, they were glad for they knew the birthday of the greatest Person in the world had come again.

One year a visiting musician heard one of the shepherd's tunes that he never forgot. He wrote it down and carried it back to his own home with him. Many people learned to sing it then, and ever since it has been played and sung around the world. Close your eyes! Listen and you will hear the shepherds' music that has traveled so far. You may see the shepherds in your mind as you hear the tune they played for Jesus' birthday. ("Doing Friendly Things" is played.)

Jesus had friends who liked to go for walks with him. They remembered what he talked about for they listened so carefully they could tell to others what he said. The stories were written down by Matthew, Mark, Luke, and John; and we love to read them.

Once when his friends were having a quarrel, Jesus asked, "What is the matter?" They were ashamed to tell him. Each one had wanted to be more important than all the rest, so they said to Jesus, "Who is the greatest one?" In our song is the answer. Find it.

Read the two stanzas. Wait for the children's retorts and their explanation of "conquerors" and "hero host." Before singing call

105

attention to the prolonged stress on "kings" and on the first syllable of *"peo*-ple" so that the rhythm is maintained throughout.

DOING FRIENDLY THINGS

Marion Brown Shelton   Adapted from a Neapolitan Tune

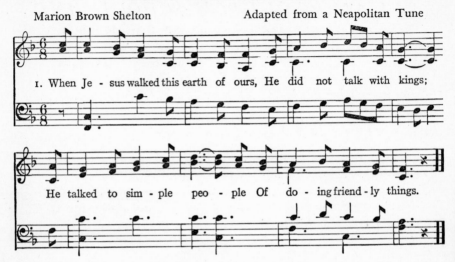

1. When Je - sus walked this earth of ours, He did not talk with kings; He talked to sim - ple peo - ple Of do - ing friend - ly things.

2 He did not praise the conquerors,
And all their hero host,
He said the very greatest
Were those who loved the most.

Words by Marion Brown Shelton. Copyright, The Pilgrim Press. Used by permission. Music from *Sing, Children, Sing,* copyright 1939 by Edith Lovell Thomas, No. 102. Used by permission of Abingdon-Cokesbury Press.

CHAPTER VIII

RELATING CHURCH SCHOOL AND CHOIR MUSICAL EXPERIENCES
(For Juniors and Teen-agers Especially)

Gladly to the house of worship come we today,
Thanks to give for quiet churches where people pray;
For the organ music sounding far off and near;
For the high sun-lighted windows, colored or clear.

Some delight in country chapel built on a hill;
Others kneel in great cathedral dimlit and still;
Temple congregations sing the Psalms loved of yore;
All are set apart for worship, God to adore.[1]

THE sense of belonging is a deep need of every child as of every adult. As soon as one is old enough to sing in a group, he begins to draw satisfaction from the common heritage which is his as a member of society. The music that his spiritual fathers accumulated is a rich deposit and one of the most accessible of his possessions. The "perpetual hopes" of the great religious traditions are celebrated with peculiar power in poetry and music. These arts suggest the unseen and the real with compelling clarity.

The junior and teen-ager, being good "joiners" and keen about all lively and lovely things, are ready to enter with comrades into choir activities even though they have had no taste of them earlier. These express and cement for them more effectively, their relationship with the religious community. Through the choir their desire to belong can be fulfilled.

How a true ministry of music can be performed is hard to see without the educational training which an intelligent and systematic choir affords. In it are learned the best hymn resources of the ages and the art of singing them with understanding. Under its direction

[1] Copyright 1935 by Edith Lovell Thomas.

opportunity is granted to offer musical service in public worship, and the individual is initiated into the widest, most stimulating fellowship known to human beings—the Christian Church.

Worship, highest of all arts, demands long, diligent study and practice. Children and youth through choir auspices have opened to them tried disciplines where the art of worship is cultivated under competent teachers. Culture of the religious spirit in the impressionable young person is nurtured through the release of his finest emotions—love, joy, aspiration—on the wings of music. To deny him this outlet is to choke the very springs of his inner life at their source.[2]

Close correlation of the music taught in the choir with the curriculum the choristers are studying in their church school is an imperative commonly disregarded. Sometimes the two programs are rivals or even opposed to each other. How the singers function as live worshipers in both church and school is a responsibility that rests squarely on the shoulders of music leaders and teachers. Rewarding results come only from careful, co-operative planning. Without this boys and girls receive fragmentary impressions due to disparate efforts and unco-ordinated fare.

To get at the need for integration of materials, sharing of purposes, and working together for satisfying experiences firsthand information has been sought through personal correspondence. Recent reports, in printed or mimeographed form, of attempts to deal with the problem also are quoted to shed light on its solution.

Excerpts from replies to letters show concern over what is happening to junior and teen-age groups when blind guides are in charge, or because enlightened foresight is not present. This situation apparently has received slight attention. Now, however, anxiety over it is expressed and efforts to alter it are beginning to be made.

Music, a Meeting Place for Juniors and Adults

Here is an encouraging story from a teacher:

In a vacation school the juniors were using a unit on the church. In the course of our study we went to visit a Negro church. The minister of that church told us how the congregation had come to have their church and explained some of the symbols. He told us that his congregation loved to sing. We told him that we had learned to sing the Spiritual, "Lord, I want to be a Christian,"

[2] Edith Lovell Thomas, "The Junior Choir," *Religious Education,* September-October, 1949.

at vacation school and asked if he would sing it with us. He replied that he usually depended on the choir and since some of the women were in the kitchen that morning, preparing a dinner, he would ask them to come in and sing with us. They came in quietly. Soon the church rang with the music of the Spiritual. It was beautiful. In talking over our visit the juniors agreed that the nicest part had been when they sang with the choir at the church.[3]

Separation Between Choir and School Experiences

A director of religious education expresses her view:

I am afraid I have not yet made much progress in such a relationship. About the only time I see a glimmer of light is when a special service, such as Student Day, is in the offing, or those days directly related to religious education, and then I have liberty to make suggestions in conference with the organist. By and large, however, the junior and high school choirs are much too apart from the rest of the church school experience. There is certainly a tremendous field to be developed in this relation. I *wish* that organists and directors might come closer together for more integrated planning.[4]

From the angle of a state-wide worker:

I wish that I could cite right off some wonderful work being done in our state between the church school and church music leadership. I am not able at this moment to give you any instances where there is careful thought given on the part of both groups to this phase of church life. Usually the church school people go ahead on their own and the choir leader selects persons from the departments to be formed into children's choirs.[5]

Beginnings of Integration

What have I done in the musical ministry to integrate the activities and program of choirs and church school? My quick reply would be, "Only a beginning." The four youth choirs, numbering one hundred and twenty-five, are church school choirs. No one is a member who is not an active member in the church school. We have almost perfect attendance the year through, without any awards, prizes, etc. This is due largely to an approach through the medium of worship, building concepts of God on the various age levels, so that songs, hymns, and anthems have meaning for them. The groups all seem to have a deep sense of worship, both in the church and church school. For instance, we never have the problem of whispering. No adult ever sits with them. We study together not only the music, but the meaning of the words of the anthem, which results in vital, meaningful singing, and a real worship experience.

---

[3] Mrs. Fred V. McDonnell, Carlisle, Pennsylvania.

[4] Mrs. Phyllis N. Maramarco, Hartford, Connecticut.

[5] Edith F. Welker, Associate Secretary, The Connecticut Council of Churches.

The former pastor of this church always worked with me on the worship service when the youth choirs sang—the third one of the month was their Sunday. The music of both senior and youth choirs was pertinent to the whole service.

As I work with the choirs I try to keep constantly in mind that it isn't how well they sing, though they do sing beautifully, but how fully they enter into the service of worship, and leave with a feeling of having shared as well as received.[6]

Choir and School Working in Unison

We have worked through the medium of a Saturday Choir School. The School is set up to enrich the regular Sunday Church School program and to give definite music training. In order to accomplish our purpose we have laid very careful plans. The leaders of each age group in the Sunday and Saturday Schools have met with both the Dean of the School and the Minister of Music and Education. Selection of material is made in order that each knows what the other is doing. The musical resource people, who were also at the initial meeting, then get together with the Minister of Music and Education and discuss the program of music, which, incidentally, includes choric reading material as well. All of this must correlate with the other materials being used.

Songs are selected for their melodic values and, of course, for the subject matter being taught. Scripture readings to be used in various corporate worship periods are worked out by the choric reading leaders and are taught to the children. Both the songs and the scripture selections are used in both the Sunday and the Saturday Schools.

Music is selected, for the most part, to meet the needs of the various age groups, but in cases where selections are to be used in corporate worship some suitable songs of each age level are taught to the children of all age levels. They therefore have some selections which they all know and can join in and sing together periodically.

It has been our experience that the children have responded magnificently to the program, learning very important basic philosophies set forth in the songs used. It is a startling fact that because materials to be used in corporate worship are known and understood by these children their participation in such services changes from, in some cases, chaos to dignified, meaningful worship for all participating—even in the situations where the children are sharing their worship experiences with adults in formal Sunday morning services.

Music has become among all these children a vital, living source of Christian character, I believe.[7]

[6] Grace Mary Williams, Director of Religious Education (including music), Oak Park, Illinois.

[7] Nelle Gilmore, Minister of Music and Education, Old First Presbyterian Church, San Francisco, California. Used by permission.

110

Big Harvest from a Small Field

"Christian Character Through Children's Choirs" is the subject of the September, 1950, issue of *Choristers Guild Letter*, edited by Ruth Krehbiel Jacobs. She introduces an exciting tale with:

We expect big churches to do big things but when little churches do big things, it is news. This is the story of the circuit rider. He serves five little churches, none of which could afford to hire a music director. He has boundless energy and his sincerity is matched only by his enthusiasm; but most of all he has simplicity. And that is why the five little churches have created something bigger than themselves. Here is his story in his own words:

After attending a Summer Choir School we were so filled with the desire to do things that we came back to our little church in Pottsgrove, Pennsylvania, determined to put into effect the things we had been taught. We organized a senior choir and a junior choir. The senior choir men didn't even know where the bass part of the music was but they were willing to try and because of their willingness to try a miracle was performed in this little church of one hundred people. A choir of sixty voices came into being. The church membership doubled, the Sunday school doubled, we were able to buy a new organ, redecorate the church, put in a P. A. system, and now the spirit of joy is throughout this church.

Another little country church called Paradise Reformed Church, became inquisitive and wanted to find out what was happening here. It now has two nice choirs, a lovely organ, and a beautifully decorated church. In both these country churches the junior choirs have put on recitals and the senior choirs have sung cantatas at Christmas and at Easter.

Then some of the urban churches became inquisitive and we are now serving three churches in Milton, Pennsylvania, besides the two country churches. In the First Presbyterian Church of Milton, where there was one choir of twelve voices, we now have four vested choirs of one hundred voices. The First Evangelical Church had no choir when we started. Now it has a vested choir of one hundred and ten voices. In both these churches we have put the multiple choir system into effect. In St. John's Reformed Church we have three vested choirs and hope to have a fourth one before long.

You may say, "Well, what makes these people come?" We firmly believe that not only should we give the best of music for the worship of God in our church but we also need some time for play. We plan parties and entertainments for all our choirs. A social program for all of them goes on throughout the year, sometimes in individual choirs, sometimes all churches cooperating, and once or twice a year all the junior, youth and adult choirs come together for a music festival. This is a great occasion.

This thing can be done in any locality if a person has the will to do it. All I have had is a knowledge of singing plus what I have gained in summer schools.

But I am not going to let it rest there. I am beginning the study of harmony, theory, dictation and music appreciation so that I will have the very foundation of music and can be of much greater service to my choirs and community.[8]

Choir as Part of Church School

Where real progress is being made:

Music is many times a means of spiritual interpretation that succeeds where nothing else can. I find that all children love music and can do something about it—give it out in some way. Every child should have that opportunity and pleasure and we are trying to make it possible here on Sunday morning.

We have three choirs: a third grade choir taking in the entire class of twenty children, a junior choir of about thirty girls and a junior high choir of twenty-five boys and girls. I can't get the junior boys interested yet. Each choir serves the needs of the children of its age range and all choirs are attended enthusiastically and voluntarily. It is all a part of our session from nine-thirty to twelve. This makes our choirs belong to the religious education program of the church school and not something extra-curricular.

I believe that every director of religious education should have a thorough training in music. If it hasn't been possible every advantage should be taken to get musical knowledge and appreciation. Most churches can't afford a minister of children's music. The combination of religious education and music is ideal for church school work.

The junior high choir likes to do things perfectly and is thrilled when they believe themselves to have reached perfection. The group responses are wonderful and the enthusiasm contagious. We are giving a concert on a Sunday afternoon and are taking up a collection to pay for some new robes. This is a healthy project. Many junior high boys and girls have said, "We come to church on Sunday because we like the choir most."

Their choir period lasts forty-five minutes and comes just before the church service. They attend church together in a group to "help the minister with the singing," they say. All three choirs are asked to sing in church frequently, sometimes separately, sometimes jointly or antiphonally with the adult choir." [9]

Adapting Plans to People

A young man who is in charge of the youth choirs and the religious education program expresses the needs as he sees them and tells how the church workers are co-operating to meet them.

All music in the church, particularly that relating to the children and young people, is and should be a part of the total Christian education work of the

---

[8] W. C. Mathius in *Choristers Guild Letter.* Used by permission.

[9] Mrs. Miriam Gorton, Director of Religious Education, The Neighborhood Church, Pasadena, California.

church. With that in mind this after-school religious training program activity was formulated with two primary needs to be met: (1) It was felt that in our situation we needed to be conducting some type of weekday religious training program, since all religious education has been taken from the public schools. (2) It was becoming increasingly difficult to get boys and girls to rehearsals on Saturdays or after school because of many school and civic activities.

Our after-school club embraces all children of the junior and intermediate departments. The boys and girls of our church, Sunday school, and surrounding community come immediately after school to the church one day a week from 3:30 to 7:00. The class work is somewhat similar to that of a vacation church school and we use vacation and weekday texts as a curriculum guide. The other phase of the club is the choir program. The music for the choirs is selected to correlate as closely as possible with the general units of work in the whole program. Besides the anthems that the choirs prepare for worship services a program of hymn education is carried out.

The first activity is a general recreational and movie period which lasts until 4:30. This allows for the children to come in at various times from many schools throughout the city. At 4:30 the groups go to their respective activities. At the close of the first period dinner is served for all ages in the assembly room. This is a well-balanced meal served by the mothers at cost (approximately 40 cents). Mealtime is also good for fun-singing and fellowship. The third period is like the second period except in reverse.

The enthusiasm for such an organization can be truly inspiring to any church and its workers. In the first year of this club we experienced an enrollment almost as large as the corresponding departments in the Sunday church school and an average attendance in many classes of around 95%.[10]

One church reports on its Sunday evening "School for Living." The plan is similar to that of the "After-School Club" where groups of different ages divide into classes. The minister of music rotates from week to week, teaching each group in turn to understand what the ministry of music is, how every person is to serve and to be served through it. The hymnal and its great resources are brought in, and some of its undiscovered riches are explored. Real growth in this expanding church fellowship through musical means is already seen after only a few weeks of earnest application of this plan. The main objective is stated in these words:

The thing that we are trying to do in our music program is to make church music live for everybody who is touched by it in our church. . . . We are trying to co-ordinate it so that children and grownups will not think of it as music

[10] Donald R. Mathis, First Federated Church, Peoria, Illinois, in *Choristers Guild Letter.* Used by permission.

for their special group, but music of *our church*. That is why we teach children from the hymnal as well as from their own departmental books.[11]

"Announcing the Ministry of Music"

Quotations from a folder, carrying a picture of the church, sent out by a Minister of Music to the parish when he began his work:

The ministry of music as we envision it . . . first, the preparation and presentation in the worship services of such religious music as is worthy of being offered up to Almighty God and of being shared with those who make up the fellowship of the church. We believe that this music should be selected and performed not as an end in itself but always with the objective of more meaningful worship for all who attend the service.

The second purpose . . . is related to enriching the church-centered experiences of the children and adults in our fellowship. . . . Through rehearsals and lessons and whatever other means are available we hope to provide many opportunities for individual growth and expression . . . through that participation not only to be better persons and more effective Christians but to add significantly to the strength and witness of our church.

The church which carries on this ministry is one of the ever growing number of churches throughout the land who are making it possible for boys and girls to enjoy choral participation from pre-school days on into adulthood . . . that the Psalmist's injunction may become a reality: "Let the people praise thee, O God; let ALL the people praise thee." [12]

The motivation of the project, the program proposed, and what the church members can do to participate complete the statement about "serving to build a singing church!"

Mr. Moyer, the builder directing this enterprise, writes in a personal letter:

We are especially interested in unifying the musical programs of the various choirs and church school departments so that neither activity will be placed in a separate pigeon hole in the child's experience. . . . We use the various age choirs to lead worship in their own departments once a month so that the program is constantly being stimulated by short time goals which, one by one, are being reached. . . .

On the results in the lives of singers and in the church these are a few of the convictions that have been formed by my particular experience: choir members

[11] Mrs. Madeline D. Ingram, Minister of Music, Memorial Methodist Church, Lynchburg, Virginia, and Professor of Church Music, Lynchburg College.

[12] J. Edward Moyer, Minister of Music, Hamline Methodist Church, Washington, D.C., and Professor of Church Music, Westminster Theological Seminary. Used by permission.

have a higher sense of reverence because they have been sensitized to beauty, dignity and propriety in worship. . . . [They] come to feel at home in the church because they have an intimate and significant task to prepare for and perform. They belong! The ministry of music is an effective means of evangelization. . . . More young people come into the choir first, then join the church, than vice versa. Some of these were personality types that probably would not have been won over by the most excellent preaching, but who responded to personal friendship, a specific task to perform and the sense of being needed. The ministry of music with no paid soloists has the highest morale and is best able to present . . . truly "church music" not simply "music in church." [13]

"Goals for Youth Choirs"

Toward which the training is aiming:
To build eternal values into the life of each child.
Through music and instruction basic Christian beliefs are taught. Music as a means of religious education is stressed.

To teach reverence and worship. The children are taught the significance of the various parts of the worship service, the meaning of the churchly appointments in the sanctuary, and how to conduct themselves at worship.

To teach correct basic habits in singing. Good posture, deep breathing, ease in singing and correct pronunciation are stressed in each rehearsal.

To assist in bringing the child to a place of musical literacy. Supplementing the training the child receives elsewhere the elements of musical notation and sight-reading are taught.

To train the child in self-discipline and co-operation. In a choir all must work together for the good of a worthy cause. This takes self-control, faithfulness and submission to appointed leadership.

To teach the great hymns and anthems of the church. An effort is made to teach "music they will grow into, not music they will out-grow," music the children will sing and cherish in a lifetime of Christian living.

To prepare and present music for occasional services and special musical programs through which the congregation may worship God. The children not only learn the music but they are instructed in the deportment which is becoming to worship leaders.[14]

Words of Encouragement

Ruth Krehbiel Jacobs sends out a monthly *Choristers Guild Letter* to choir leaders, subscribers from many states, which contains practical help for the small or large church. Out of her wide experi-

---

[13] *Ibid.*

[14] From *Music Department Prepares for Active Season,* Highland Park Methodist Church, Dallas, Texas. Dr. Federal Lee Whittlesey, Minister of Music; Rev. Marshall T. Steel, Minister. Used by permission.

ence, plus contributions from others, come cheering thoughts and provocative suggestions. She asks:

Do you sometimes become discouraged when you compare your work with that of larger and more prominent churches? Take heart—you are not responsible for the larger crop that grows in the vineyard across the way. You *are* responsible for every grape in your own. The measure of your success is the adequacy with which you meet the conditions that exist in your own church: nowhere else. No two directors have quite the same problems or the same opportunities. You can learn from others. You cannot successfully imitate. Every fine achievement is the result of good judgment in matching a procedure to a specific situation. It takes imagination, courage and common sense to build and hold a good choir. The practice of all three will hurt no one.[15]

Mrs. Jacobs urges musical advance in Christian education by asking us to attempt the impossible instead of surrendering to the thought, "It can't be done here." She declares:

The choirs represent too small a part of the church school and the church school is too small for the church. It is our responsibility and it should be our purpose as individual directors to change that situation. To do it we must have a sense of mission. We must be apostles of the impossible. The pattern of the impossible:
  1. Each child in the parish a regular member of the church school;
  2. Each child in the church school receiving training in music and worship;
  3. A choir in every church school;
  4. A dedicated and educated director for every choir.[16]

Interviews with Choir Directors

Three alumni of Union Theological Seminary School of Sacred Music, sensitive to the influence of music on the people in their choirs answer direct questions put to them.

Question: What changes do you see taking place in the lives of the singers?

There is the matter of identification of singers, younger and older, with the church. I have seen it happen . . . where a child's entry into the church is a splendid potential threshold for an entire family's renewed interest in the church.

There is . . . a new respect for the demands of worship. A singer who prepares intensively for a service will not take the service lightly.

I feel, too, that a good musical setting is one of the best ways of planting a devotional text in the heart of a child.

[15] *Choristers Guild Letter,* April, 1950. Used by permission.
[16] *Ibid.*

I am discovering how valuable a deliberate devotional effort in rehearsals can be. We always have "devotions" in our rehearsals and I think they point up our musical efforts.[17]

Question: Can you cite an instance of a difference the choir has made in the life of one individual child?

Our most successful efforts have been the result of personal touches. A new ten-year-old boy joined the choir. He was endowed with a natural physical poise and grace which led the other children to choose him to lead the processionals. His musical interest was indifferent—in fact he seemed slightly scornful of the whole business. At Thanksgiving time I rather impulsively sent him a note complimenting him and his pace in the processional and told him he had timed it exactly to my satisfaction. The next Sunday his parents wrung my hand and told me I would never know what I had done for their son. . . . His very busy father during the war had to travel; the boy was parked with his grandmother for a year; in moving to this community and changing schools he was behind children of his age; public school teachers had failed to capture his imagination or stimulate a desire for improvement; in choir there was a little thing in which he excelled and he had already lost some of his surly manner.

The child carries the tattered remains of that letter in his dungaree pocket and often asks me if I remember it. His parents have convinced him that if he could do so well in one thing he can do as well in others.

I gave him the page boy solo in "Good King Wenceslas" that Christmas. People were thrilled with him. This year he volunteered for special reading classes in school and is a well-loved leader in his gang.

I don't take all the credit. He has smart parents. They claim they might have waited longer to find the peg on which to hang their program and that the choir had provided it sooner. . . . No doubt, certain intangibles of Christianity go into this too.[18]

Question: How do you try to develop character?

I rather suspect that character is developed by association with other Christian people in the work of music. Particularly would I think this is true in the field of young people. My observation here is that they get more by association than they get by formal suggestions or activity.

I find that the more thorough I am in the musical preparation, the more complete is the spiritual understanding of the work. A comprehensive spiritual understanding has overtones which show in the development of interest in

---

[17] Dr. Donald D. Kettring, Minister of Music, East Liberty Presbyterian Church, Pittsburgh, Pennsylvania. Author of *Steps Toward a Singing Church.*

[18] William Davis, formerly Minister of Music, Hillside Presbyterian Church, Orange, New Jersey.

the music program. I cannot stress too thoroughly the need which I feel for complete musical preparation before one attacks the emotional problems and understanding of the text itself. The spiritual expression of music is only available to those who have accomplished and thoroughly understood the technical aspects and the preparations required for performance.[19]

Question: Is it wise to have juniors and intermediate singers rehearse together?

We do not have enough to divide. Therefore our big girls sit with the juniors and help with finding the line in the music and in seeing that breathing and phrasing are pencilled in correctly. The juniors seem thrilled to have the big girls give notice to them. We have fun, not by racing around in games, but by really enjoying the music. I do not hesitate to point out beauties of pure sound, lovely melody, clear and radiant harmony, and the satisfying inevitability of a cadence. Likewise the words are examined for imagery. Sometimes I ask how they themselves would convey a spiritual idea and compare their ideas with the hymnwriter's. Sometimes the children produce a better and more poetic one. I have been training my juniors to sing beautiful "amens" in lovely tone quality and therein lies a certain worship experience.[20]

Question: Is interest shown by the younger singers in what the adult choir is doing?

The older juniors attend the adult choir's musical services. They wanted to usher at one wearing their vestments and I allowed it. Several older girls wanted me to go over the Brahms' "Requiem" with them after the older choir had performed it and were starry-eyed over the beauty of the music and the line, "Yea, I will comfort you as one whom his own mother comforteth." They hope the choir will still be singing it when they will be old enough to join the adults. I was glad that they sensed that there are marvelous things to grow into.[21]

In printed orders of services, sent in by some of the ministers of music quoted above, these junior and youth choir anthems appear. First lines of hymns, in most instances well known, which stress the same, or similar, thoughts, are added to indicate how church and church school worship is, or can be, integrated with choir learnings, or vice versa.

[19] W. Frederic Miller, now Minister and formerly Director of Music, First Presbyterian Church, Youngstown, Ohio.
[20] William Davis, *op. cit.*
[21] *Ibid.*

Junior and Youth Choir Anthems	*Correlative Hymns and Songs*
1. Adam, A., "O Holy Night" (Christmas)	"Silent Night"
2. Austrian Carol: Clarence Dickinson, "Shepherds' Christmas Song"	"While Shepherds Watched Their Flocks"
3. Bach, J. S., "Come Together, Let Us Sing"	"Rejoice, Ye Pure in Heart"
4. Bach, J. S.: Clarence Dickinson, "O Saviour Sweet"	"Fairest Lord Jesus"
5. Bohemian Carol, "Let Our Gladness Know No End"	"Joy to the World"
6. Bohemian Carol, "We Bring You Glad Tidings"	"The First Noel"
7. Brother James' Air: Gordon Jacobs, "The Lord's My Shepherd"	"O God, Our Help" (Psalm Paraphrase)
8. Curry, W. Lawrence, "St. Richard's Prayer"	"Father in Heaven, Who Lovest All"
9. Dickinson, Clarence: arranged from a spiritual folk song, "A Song in Praise of the Lord of Heaven and Earth"	"All Creatures of Our God"
10. Dickinson, Clarence, "Easter Anthem"	"O Joyous Easter Morning" (with tune, "My Heart Ever Faithful": J. S. Bach)
11. Dickinson, Clarence, "Grace Before Singing" ("God of all lovely sounds")	"When Morning Gilds the Skies"
12. Dickinson, Clarence (Westminster Chimes' Theme), "List to the Lark" ("Praise God for work, food, rest")	"We Gather Together to Ask the Lord's Blessing"
13. Farjeon, Harry, "Now Every Child That Dwells on Earth Stand Up and Sing" (Christmas)	"Good Christian Men, Rejoice"
14. Hebrew Liturgy Antiphon: Clarence Dickinson, "Adoration"	"Let the Words of My Mouth Be Acceptable unto Thee"
15. Hebrew Melody: Harvey Gaul, "Hear, O Israel"	"The God of Abram Praise," or "O Come, O Come, Emmanuel"
16. Kettring, Donald, "Come, Let Us Worship God"	"Now Thank We All Our God"
17. Kopolyoff, "Alleluia! Christ Is Risen"	"Christ the Lord Is Risen Today," or "The Strife Is O'er, Alleluia" (with tune, "Victory": Palestrina)
18. Moravian Liturgy: Roberta Bitgood, "Hosanna" (Palm Sunday)	"All Glory, Laud, and Honor to Christ"

19. Ochs, Siegfried (wrongly attributed to Handel), "Thanks Be to Thee" — "My God, I Thank Thee Who Hast Made the Earth" (with tune, "Fowler": Robert G. McCutchan)

20. Roberton, Hugh, "Let All the World in Every Corner Sing" — Same text with hymn tune

21. Seventeenth Century: Jungst, "While Shepherds Watched" (Christmas) — "There's a Song in the Air"

22. Shaw, Geoffrey, "Worship" ("O brother man, fold to thy heart thy brother") — Same text with hymn tune

23. Shaw, Martin, "With a Voice of Singing" — "With Happy Voices Ringing"

24. Thiman, Eric, "A Seasonal Thanksgiving" — "We Plow the Fields"

25. Welsh Air: Katherine Davis, "A Song of Thanksgiving" ("Let all things now living unite in thanksgiving") — "Come, Ye Thankful People"

To amplify above list, a few other selections are added.

26. Bach, J. S.: Clarence Dickinson, "God, My Shepherd, Walks Beside Me" — "A Mighty Fortress Is Our God' (Psalm Paraphrase)

27. Bach, J. S., "My Heart Ever Faithful, Sing Praises, Be Joyful" — "Joyful, Joyful, We Adore Thee"

28. Dvorak, A.: J. Julius Baird, "God Is My Shepherd" — "The King of Love My Shepherd Is"

29. Franck, C.: Bryceson Treharne, "O Lord Most Holy" — "Holy, Holy, Holy, Is the Lord of Hosts" (from Cantata, "The Holy City")

30. German Carol: Gustav Holst, "Christmas Song" — "We Three Kings of Orient Are"

31. Jewish Tune: Charlotte Lockwood, "Men and Children Everywhere" — "Rock of Ages, let our song praise thy saving power" (with the same tune for "The Feast of Lights," chapter I)

32. "Praxis Pietatis": Katherine Davis, "Praise to the Lord, the Almighty" — Same text with hymn tune

33. Roberton, Hugh, "All in an April Evening" (Good Friday) — "Into the Woods My Master Went"

EVALUATE AND CORRELATE HYMNS AND ANTHEMS

This session may well culminate in sharing information about hymns and anthems which in the group's judgment are sung most worshipfully by young choirs or departments in their services. Here is a chance to harvest and exchange a sheaf of new numbers.

Classify selections to make sure that they represent types of music that fit the requirements of the singers and give knowledge of significant church song, while interpreting the Christian religion as it is being learned in the church school. Keep in mind the main outcome to be realized by means of singing—the experience of worship in the lives of the boys and girls who make the music.

Work through an exercise in analysis. Set down major emphases of a curriculum, designed to foster Christian living among juniors and teen-agers. Accent these objectives by your choice of songs, hymns, and anthems which embody such concepts and lift them by music to a high emotional plane.

As a basis use the list on pages 119-20, or other numbers brought in by the class and you may come out with an evaluation of this kind:

Basic Values Sought	Distinctive Types of Music	a—Anthems b—Hymns, Songs
Familiarity with life of Jesus; feeling kinship with him	Carol	a. 1, 2, 5, 6, 30 b. 1, 4, 6, 12, 13, 30
Know biblical language of devotion	Psalm Tune	a. 7 b. 2, 5, 7
Practice act of adoration	Liturgical: Hebrew, Moravian, etc.	a. 14, 18 b. 14, 29
Expression of joy through singing	Chorale	a. 3, 4, 20, 26, 31 b. 3, 9, 27
Have concern for others	(1) Sacred Chorus (2) Hymn Tune	a. 22 (1) b. 22 (2)
Celebrate holy days in sincerity	(1) Anthem (2) Folk Song	a. 1, 10, 17, 24 b. 4
Give self to God in serving people	Choral Response or Introit	a. 11 b. 14
Sense of unity with every race and nation	Historic melodies from many peoples	a. 31 b. 26
Awareness of the presence of God in individuals, great servants of mankind, for example, Johann Sebastian Bach, father of Protestant church music	Solo and Beautiful Harmonies, etc.	a. 26, 27 b. 10
Feeling security with God for companion	Descant or Counter Melody	a. 7, 26

121

CHAPTER IX

GUIDED BY INSPIRING LEADERS

Let thy day be to thy night
A teller of good tidings. Let thy praise
Go up as birds go up that, when they wake,
Shake off the dew and soar.
    So take Joy home,
And make a place in thy great heart for her,
And give her time to grow, and cherish her.[1]

OUR study in foregoing chapters has been based on the assumption that those in charge of the educational program because of their Christian faith both practice the worship of God and are seriously concerned to help children and youth under their care build sound habits of devotion.

Whatever phases and methods of education are being considered, foremost in mind and underlying all are the claims of worship. If worship's importance seems to be slighted or pushed aside in the discussion, it should be brought back into the center of our thinking.

What is the main function of leaders, their supreme service that must be rendered to justify their being employed? Is it not to stimulate a living, loving relationship between individuals and God through every means at their disposal, a relationship reflected in sincere worship attitudes and expressions? In particular how shall the delight and discipline of musical training contribute to that main outcome as the program is planned and conducted?

A starting point is the belief in the universal presence of music within persons and the faith that it awakens to stimuli of the highest order. Walt Whitman, confident of this fact and its potentiality, writes:

All music is what awakes from you when you are reminded by the instruments,
It is not the violins and the cornets . . . the oboe . . . the beating drums . . . the

[1] Jean Ingelow: "Dominion."

baritone . . . the men's chorus . . . the women's chorus,
It is nearer and farther than they.[2]

The leader by the favorable choice of music, and having it well done, is to bring to life what is fine within each individual—reverence, gratitude for the sense of God—when reminded by makers of instruments, composers, players, and most persuasive of all, the human voice.

The music is indeed nearer to us than what we hear, for

> I opened the doors of my heart,
>   And behold,
> There was music within
>   And a song! [3]

A knock on the door of the heart, or someone to push it ajar, is what it takes to awaken the music within.

The music is indeed farther than what we hear, for it speaks to us words from God when we give it undivided attention. When it touches our imagination, we explore a new world, drawn by its voice.

Three parties are involved in every musical transaction—those who create, those who present, and those who receive. The delivery of goods is not completed until each party has done his share.

How this exchange takes place is visualized and promoted by the intelligent leader. It follows somewhat this pattern when applied to an anthem, for instance, as a means of worship:

Selection

If the anthem is to benefit the congregation, whose participation in it is passive rather than active, it must be a worthy and sincere act of worship on the part of the choir. It is a musical meditation on high and holy things; not an entertainment for wealthy persons who hire the singers for their own pleasure. Nor must it go beyond the technical skill and the musical capacity of the singers; it should be a giving of their best, according to their real ability. . . . Corruptions of divine service may not be excused, however amiable may be the intentions of the persons concerned. . . . Choose and permit only such anthems as may be a worthy offering to God from the skilled singers of the choir.[4]

Adhering to this standard set up by a man who because of training, character, and experience is one to heed, we choose for our purpose,

---

[2] Walt Whitman, "A Song for Occupations."
[3] Jean Ingelow, "Dominion."
[4] Winfred Douglas, *op. cit.,* p. 140.

"Lead Me, Lord," a brief, simple anthem by Samuel Sebastian Wesley, grandson of the hymn writer Charles Wesley. When sacred music had fallen to a low level, this composer lifted it to a place of integrity and force. With directness his music urges the prayer of the Psalmist: "Lead me, O Lord, in thy righteousness, . . . make thy way straight before my face: for thou, Lord, only, makest me dwell in safety." [5]

Preparation

The counsel given to young Timothy regarding his ministry applies equally to choristers charged with the solemn yet joyous ministry of musical worship: "Do your best to present yourself to God as one approved, a workman who has no need to be ashamed, rightly handling the word of truth." [6]

The choir is cautioned, "See that thou believest in thy heart what thou singest with thy mouth; and approve in thy works what thou believest in thy heart." This charge was a portion of the ordination of singers in early church days.

The anthem is begun by a girl or woman with a low subdued voice, or the altos in unison, being entrusted with opening the door of the sanctuary, as it were. The request is made for guidance in the bewildering path of life, sung in the first person in a tune of chantlike simplicity. There are exactly eight pronouns in the first person and eight addressed to God. These should be sung with clarity to underline the personal nature of the petition. The whole choir reinforces the soloist by repeating the request—the sopranos reproducing the melody in the same low register while the other voices support it with harmony.

One soprano, or more, in the second section declares confidence in the security which comes only from God. The phrase rises to its height on "dwell" and descends to a serene close. This theme is taken up by the entire choir, confessing again the faith common to all who rely upon the "everlasting arms."

By "the practice of the presence of God" the choristers articulate their desires. They prepare themselves definitely to speak for the people with more urgency, perhaps, than the people can express their aspirations, underscoring the thoughts with music.

[5] Psalm 5:8; 4:8 K.J.V.
[6] II Timothy 2:15 R.S.V.

Presentation

This particular anthem is an easy one, by which either a small or larger church can usher in a service for people who range from juniors to adults, or for group-graded worship, where only younger choirs usually function.

The organ or piano supplies an unobtrusive background so that the words of prayer can be understood as all absorb its spirit. No soloist who tries to perform the priestly act allows himself to get between the music and the hearers. His aim is to point the way to worship not to be heard for his voice production or to attract attention to himself as leader.

Singing the number from memory will mean more thorough learning and correspondingly carries more weight with those who receive the impression. The spirit of earnestness which imbues the messengers is contagious. One should never expect a generous response to an effort that has been sparing.

Before entering the sanctuary ministers and choirs often pray together that they may act as one in the service they perform. This can easily be made mere routine and is no substitute for adequate study and training. However, when not only the minister leads, but the director and choristers take their turns, sincere group prayer can be transmuted into power to lift the congregation through word and music.

Reception

People awake to the privilege of prayer provided by the church when reminded by sacred music thus sounded. In the silence of the heart they respond to the sung prayer and give assent to its aspiring faith. Attending to the summons they become one in purpose, fitted to engage in Christian fellowship, not as recipients only, but actively completing the threefold work of creator, performer, and listener.

Trace the give and take operation through from start to finish to see what music can arouse when used as a reminder. This is one of the arts of a true leader: from failure as from success he learns to find a surer path for those who seek to worship together "in spirit and truth." [7]

Let us remember that the experience of worship cannot be confined to any certain room in the church, to any fixed time, to any

[7] John 4:24 R.S.V.

one vocabulary, or to any set of forms with which our own limited knowledge is connected. Frequently, even in nursery class and kindergarten, teachers seem to have in mind a church service order when they try to foster the beginnings of religious expression in children. Unless there is a grouping of song, prayer, and Bible verses, or some such series, they feel there has been no chance for religious expression. How different in general form and order from that of the Sunday morning adult service are the usual plans of the periods for juniors and upward in church school worship? Informal are the ways of taking advantage of the mood for singing in classes, while studying, working with the hands and quietly accompanying what is being done with a prayer or thoughtful word. This can help other classes rather than disturb them, by its spontaneity and suggestive influence. From singing one hymn that speaks the children's language clearly intense religious moments can be drawn, when the leader perceives the time for it, without having other means of worship brought in. Are there musical numbers here printed having such possibilities?

Having children and youth initiated into the art of worship according to adult usage is a part of their education given by the church, but to have its design as the model for all church school practice is a serious mistake. Thought and study of how a child comes to spiritual maturity will make us look for more imaginative procedures. Perhaps we need to think of synonyms and substitutes for the words "worship" and "service" which have their historic significance. What light is given on this by psychology and religious values as we view them today? In a laboratory school of religious education one summer the teachers decided on "morning meeting" as a truer name for the period. Of course the next issue to determine was a meeting for what purpose? Purposes worth coming together for, when children draw on the resources of life, are best illustrated in practice witnessed or described for us. Here is how learning and doing once became a hymn of worship and lent meaning to later singing.

Have you ever wondered when you were singing a hymn in your church school why and how the words and music . . . say what you felt and thought at that moment? . . .

It happened that the third and fourth grade juniors of a church school chapel had been visiting other churches. One Sunday they had gone to an Episcopal church. They had arrived early and were seated in an almost empty sanctuary.

It was very still and no one spoke. They watched the worshipers as . . . they knelt in prayer. Then the organ began to play and the service was begun.

On the following Sunday in their own chapel, the juniors talked about this church and the service they attended. "It was so quiet and lovely." . . . "Each person bowed his head to pray." . . . "I liked the organ best." "Did you notice the windows? . . . so high and colored?" "Yes, one had a picture of Jesus with a lamb." "There were arches everywhere."

The leader went to the piano and began to play and sing a new hymn which began, "Gladly to the house of worship, . . ." They were quiet when she finished the first stanza. Then someone said, "It tells how we felt last Sunday and what we saw." Another requested, "Sing it again." And so they listened and learned the stanza.

Other stanzas were added to the hymn . . . after the juniors had been to a service in a synagogue, a colored Baptist church, and a Catholic church in their town. They learned of many customs of worship which are practiced by people in different churches. They observed the ways in which worshipers sang hymns and read scripture. They noticed the forms of the different buildings and the beautiful symbols to remind people of God and of Jesus and of great leaders of the church.

[The author] used the thoughts of these . . . juniors [and their teacher] and wrote a hymn that all boys and girls might sing together.[8]

"All (places visited) are set apart for worship, God to adore," was the conclusion reached. The hymn was the beginning of an ongoing experience. After thinking it over one child said, "It puts us all together."

We are unable to weigh how much the sustained, reverent music of Gounod was responsible for the impressions left by this adventure. But is it not safe to assume that without it the warmth of realization would have been cooled if not lost? Reviewing the visits through the medium of melody certainly appeared to make more real the children's feeling of oneness.

In this kind of meeting of hearts and minds the spirit of Christ is caught and communicated, "for where two or three have gathered in my name, I am there among them." [9] Unity of purpose aimed at a worthy end, recalled in a religious atmosphere by singing, is an agency of Christian education. Seeing diverse people in different places in various manners paying honor to God, who is over all, reveals our common need of him.

[8] Marion C. Armstrong, "Hymn Stories," in *Trails for Juniors.* Copyright 1950 by Pierce & Smith. Used by permission. The hymn "Houses of Worship" is in *Singing Worship,* Edith Lovell Thomas (Abingdon-Cokesbury Press).
[9] Matthew 18:20 Moffatt.

Standards and Attitudes

The kind of standards set by the young people's and adult choirs will encourage or dull the desire of the younger groups to make good music and to qualify for later choir membership. By slipshod or indifferent attitudes the older singers, unfortunately, mark down the values of church musical activities in the eyes of the younger set.

The privilege and duty of the minister, choir director, and teachers are to exalt in the minds of the children, young people, and adults—all potential choristers—the opportunity and obligation of the singing office as

1. A chance to learn to sing and to serve.
2. A responsibility to the church which provides training.
3. The satisfaction of knowing and rendering with others religious music of the finest quality.
4. The sacred calling of the ministry of worship and how to take part in it.

For the leading of a congregation in worship the choir is taught to sing with and to sing for the people in the pews. At the very beginning of the service it is their part to open the way directly into worship by entering themselves through prayerful music, as in the anthem illustration "Lead Me, Lord."

The hymn is a medium for the congregation's expression of devotion, called forth by the choir's act and appeal. What hymn shall they sing familiar enough to give outlet to their emotion and fresh enough to engage their serious thought?

Selection of vital hymns and tunes that evoke enthusiastic singing is one of the most important tasks requiring the combined judgment of minister and director and all their aides. Keeping a record of the best well-known ones, with the dates when they were sung, should prevent too frequent repetition and insure a place for the finest to be had in the year's round. Not only is appropriateness to theme, condition, and day to be thought of, but variety of emphasis, style, and inclusiveness in matter and music if the singing is done "with the spirit and . . . with the mind also." [10] We must dare to attempt new things if we are to grow in knowledge and stature as worshiping Christians. At this point young people and adults have a big role of leadership to play. How can they exercise it?

The choristers are probably the first ones to come to fuller recognition of the hymn as a major part of worship in which every person

[10] I Corinthians 14:15 R.S.V.

present is vocal, all together uniting in hearty prayer and thanksgiving. This means that hymns are to be made interesting by the director as interpreting the living experiences out of which the words and music spring. Hymns reveal glorious records of human lives transformed. Filled with the dynamic spirit which created them the leader arouses the choir's eagerness to rehearse and sing hymns and anthems so that the congregation feels their contagion.

All congregations apparently need a good deal of encouragement to use their Protestant privilege of hymn singing. The pulpit sometimes introduces a hymn with a comment on its striking content, its historic significance, citing an incident of its helpfulness or using any pointer that causes one to look at it in a new light. Altering the treatment of a much-used hymn prods interest. The organist adapts his registrations to different stanzas, contrasting their contents, and ceases playing when the choir and congregation can sing a prayer stanza more fervently without accompaniment. More arresting is a question and answer hymn when congregation and choir sing it antiphonally. A single voice or the choir alone takes different portions to aid concentrating on a message that elsewise might be overlooked. A stronger climax is reached once in a while when the soprano choristers sing an exultant descant on a final stanza.

Advance from the selections the congregation sings best to adjoining territory. One path begins with all singing the familiar tune "Coronation" to "All hail the power of Jesus' name!" On the next to the last stanza just the choir branches into the more triumphant "Miles' Lane," in which the congregation joins for the final stanza.

An unfamiliar hymn, not difficult to learn, can be quickly acquired if the choir gives the people a chance to hear one or more stanzas and draws the entire assembly in for the finish.

One church had the custom of having a "choir hymn" as a usual service item presenting a different musical setting to a familiar text or an altogether new number. This broke a trail into hitherto unknown fields.

The music director in another church selects one hymn a month which has appeal to all ages. She promotes acquaintance with the hymn by having it played for the kindergarten to listen to, teaching one stanza to the primary group, and more of it to the juniors, and so on up to the adults, who learn all of it. The minister includes it in the Sunday morning service, giving his lively comment on it. The church organizations are asked to sing it in their meetings, and

129

parents are urged to make use of it at home. Having this kind of instruction from the minister of music in the church school and her helpers once a month puts into circulation fine hymns for living and and increases interest in them.

St. Paul's Protestant Episcopal Cathedral in Boston is a memorable place to attend service because of its inspiring hymn singing. This is no casual matter but is cultivated in congregational hymn rehearsals. The people are given also a prehearing of choir anthems that are to be a part of the church service, with aids to a better understanding of these contributions. This kind of help every church can lend according to its concern over leading people in a worship service that makes a difference to all who attend.

When a church service is a unit, with its moments of awareness of the Almighty, sense of personal wrong, vision, being restored, and commitment to serve, music is a link that connects one act with the next. When this link is furnished by an organ interlude, it is made more effective by the genuine though silent co-operation of the choir. Choral responses are the singers' assent to or accent upon whatever ministry is in progress.

Besides the claims laid upon the children, young people, and adults for leadership in regular services of worship that have been mentioned, there is the sharing of their training with younger and older groups in the educational program. The more training one has had, the greater is the obligation to use it for others who have had less. A soprano soloist, for example, spent a stated series of weeks in the junior choir rehearsals to work with the boys and girls to produce good tone and to improve their singing generally.

Practical illustration of the adult choir's interest in the progress of the boys and girls is invaluable in building up the unity of all parts of the church's musical ministry. This kind of support is expected and should be definitely arranged for as regular duty.

Likewise the choristers who play piano or organ well owe to the church school departments and young choirs what they have learned by acting as accompanists. We seem content with faulty and indifferent playing for children that would disturb us if it were done for adults. Perhaps we fear to ask our best musicians to assist lest we "impose upon their time." In what way could any musical talent be invested with promise of larger return? Time schedules may be such that only short and irregular visits of the most skilled persons can be hoped for, but by all means establish such contacts when and as generously as the cause warrants.

A leader for the children's choirs, when an organist or director cannot conduct them, would naturally be looked for from among the older choristers who have received the most from the church through music instruction. Each group and department should supply apprentices for the leader, teacher and pianist so that all musical resources are tapped and trainees get the practice that they need for their own development.

A church sensitive to the need of educating its choristers to be helpers sent the teen-agers with the Minister of Music to a summer music camp where they received training in leading music and playing the piano for the singing of hymns. These high school girls were then given practice in these arts in their church school under the supervision of their Minister of Music.

This same church gives children from the younger choirs, six or eight of them at a time, the chance to help the other children in their respective church school departments when a new song is taken up. The choristers thus teach in the school as they have been taught in the choir.

In recreation, entertainment, and social functions the older choirs, as well as the younger, should take the lead in fostering the fellowship which is synonymous with being Christian. Here is a delightful phase to develop about which churches have done comparatively little. Singing-game books are plentiful containing folk music designed for all ages to have fun with on church family evenings.[11] At church suppers solo, duet, quartet, and chorus numbers are entertainment features to be provided by the choir which bring forward individual talent. Humorous, lyrical, and character selections can here present the choristers in an informal role. Leading group singing of rounds, charming folks songs, and new hymns for home and church are enterprises worthy of any good choir. These features attract parents and children alike and can furnish sheer enjoyment.

A choir took pleasure in giving once a year a program that took only a little time to work up. One evening dwelt on "I hear America singing"—cowboy, work, regional, ballad, spiritual songs.[12] Another time "Songs of Long Ago" [13] were dramatized in costume. Apprecia-

[11] A woman who has charge of small country church parties is using *Let Us Be Joyful* (Co-operative Song Service, Delaware, Ohio), a booklet of hymns, graces, folk songs, and singing games when all ages come together. She throws the words, typed on a stereopticon slide, on a screen, and supplies fun and fellowship opportunities suited to family interests.

[12] A. D. Zanzig: *Singing America* (C. C. Birchard & Co.).

[13] *Ibid.*

tion of previously unknown music within our nation and abroad was increased.

A junior choir and their parents had a rewarding time learning Stephen Foster's songs.[14] The girls in long dresses put up their hair, and the boys were rigged up in keeping with the historic period. Story backgrounds, told by the singers, put a framework about the songs. Solos, duets, and other arrangements lent variety and the audience was invited to sing in an occasional chorus. The mothers were ushers, gowned in some authentic clothes produced from attic trunks. A medley of nine Foster tunes played on records by the Andre Kostelanetz orchestra was heard as the audience was arriving. New ability was discovered, and new learnings were shared. The project brought into play more of the gifts of children and parents than had been known to exist before.

Christmas carols were the content of a program a certain church used for all the choirs and their families to inaugurate the holiday season early in December. From an evergreen tree in the center of the assembly hall radiated tables at which the company had supper together. Following that, while the mothers cleared the tables, the children and the fathers decorated the tree with balls brought by everyone who came to the party. Later each of the choirs was heard alone and all sang together in chorus or antiphonally beautiful carols. The parents were brought into the singing on the numbers they knew and on old rounds that had new words adapted to the season.

Preparing the larger and finer forms of church music within their capacity to sing is rewarding for every choir, whatever its size. At least once a year, not necessarily at Christmas or Easter, when the choice carols of the nations are being happily brought into the foreground, a major work is called for—a cantata or oratorio in part if not the whole. Every real choir owes such a presentation to its community. Where one church does not have adequate singers and resources to accomplish the work alone, to combine with other church choirs is an even better project. The undertaking may be the right occasion for guest soloists to add importance and finish to the production.

The choir festival that embraces all the community choral groups, both adult and younger, or held for two or more graded ages, is a newer mode of interdenominational fellowship that choirs every-

---

[14] Obtainable at five- and ten-cent stores.

where are finding most inspiring. In this are unlimited possibilities to be tried out every season by way of practicing unity, learning finer music, and reaching higher levels of group musical expression.

With this bare outline to start you thinking set down the musical assets of your choristers and estimate how the training to be had in your church is turning them to account. In another column list the returns you are receiving from them in service and leadership. Work out how this can be improved and enlarged in a third column.

The singers cannot be held solely responsible for a lack of devotion, quality of output, and range of activities. But they are the people upon whom you depend as you affect the religious life of your entire church through musical means. A clear picture of how this can be done is a number-one outcome which this study should stir you to achieve for your church.

The organist-director of the choir is the dynamo which is the driving power for the choral services. He will not rest until co-ordinated with him are all the forces that can forward what needs to be done through right use of music.

Does your organist take care of his instrument, seeing that it and all pianos in use are protected and kept in tune? If they are inferior instruments, is he working toward getting better ones? Are they reserved for his own playing only or utilized also by adults and youths to practice on, improving their gifts and serving the church? Are the instruments played for the "glory of God and the re-creation of his people"? Does the player perfect his art for this sacred end? What quality of music is played? How varied are the numbers to suit the needs of the people, conditions, and occasions? What impressions do the congregation and the children of the church school receive through listening to the instrumental portions of the service? Can these selections be concretely described? Do you know their titles and composers? What requests are made and is appreciation given to him regarding the music offered?

As an accompanist does the organist paint in a background for singers or is the foreground blurred and confused by a too prominent organ part?

During congregational singing does the voice of the organ blend to encourage spirited singing? Does it move at a sluggish pace? Is the strain of trying to match volume and speed too much for the people to attempt? How often does the organist contribute to the education of children, youth, and adults through music chosen with a particular age in mind? What personal relations are cultivated

133

between the one who plays the organ and those who hear its music? Friends in the pews need to be conferred with if an organist is to find out just how his playing sounds to them, for his ears can rarely, if ever, get the full effect of the music he makes. Are critical comments made to the organist or to others? What influence do the comments exert?

When the specifications are made out for the musical director every church is looking for, they sound as idealistic and all-inclusive as the dreams of a person regarding a marriage mate. However, there are certain qualifications that a director should possess if choristers are to be entrusted to his care. Would the requisites you hold out for be anything like these?

1. Regard for individuals
2. Ability to work constructively with people of different ages
3. Training sufficient to command respect
4. Understanding of worship values and ability to get them expressed
5. Knowledge of sacred music resources
6. Educational approach through the entire ministry of church music
7. Consecration to the task

The piano is the instrument used commonly for church school and frequently for church worship. Comparatively few are the teachers I have known who instruct their pupils in the art of playing hymns, which requires skill and much practice. Certain points to attend to are fingering that connects tones with a smooth legato touch in each of the voices of four-part harmony. This bears watching when the tenor notes, too far from the bass to be taken by the left hand, have to be played by the right hand. The left may have to assist the right hand for a similar reason. An organ teacher used to write "H. H.," meaning "hands help," at such spots to insure smooth going. Phrasing to conform to thoughts expressed by carrying over or separating the words involved; adjusting the volume and tempo to the singing group; preserving the correct rhythm and movement to keep the exercise alive; bringing out the melody and keeping the harmony subservient to it; rendering as written rather than adding flourishes—runs, extra chords, or other distracting pianistic displays —are a few marks of good piano accompanying. A safe caution is, never play hymns without preparing yourself by practice. Request piano teachers to make hymn playing a part of their lesson plans and give to those who play for your groups your own assistance here.

Get the feel of the rhythm first, be able to carry the tune second, and hear the harmony as well-blended accompanying sound last are steps for the pianist to take who helps singers to learn a new piece of music.

With reference to utilizing other instruments questions are to be raised: Has the violinist, flutist, or other player something that is really good to give and worth hearing by the group? Will this provide an essential rather than be a substitute for singing? A fifth-grade girl, now taking lessons for the second season, plays a Bach aria very creditably for the juniors as they assemble before the hour for rehearsal. This is the time when several children volunteer to share their latest "pieces" with the others. The leader asks, "Can you play it while the children sing 'The Glad Time'?" This poem has been joined to the Bach aria for a Christmas song.[15] "I've never done that before," she says, but is delighted to try it. It works out successfully with timing and accuracy improving as she attempts it more than once. The choir picks up the tune and words quickly because of its charm, and they concentrate well, being led by one of their number. A boy brought his clarinet to show that he had learned to play "Silent Night" with his school orchestra. Although he had made progress in handling the instrument, errors in rhythm, melody, and intonation had to be corrected before he could help the group to sing. His failure to measure up to playing with the choir was a learning not missed by the boys and girls.

An old gentleman, looking back on a long life of working in the church, said, "I would never have gotten into the kingdom of God but by my fiddle." In his youth he was asked to play his violin in church during a period when such an innovation was not usually countenanced as befitting worship. Are there people in your parish deprived because of prejudice of this nature? What entrance to life does music in your church swing open to them? Does an obbligato to an anthem or an offertory number which can aid the musical education of the church school children make an opportunity for budding players in your scheme for the year?

Before making experiments in inspiring others to sing, suppose the class pauses to recall the leaders they remember who revealed to them the splendor of the Christian religion along the path of music. We seldom recollect clearly *what* we have been taught, but without exception, doubtless, our memories dwell on those persons who brought to us abundant life. Refreshed by the thought of

[15] Edith Lovell Thomas, *Sing, Children, Sing* (Abingdon-Cokesbury Press), No. 69.

what has been conferred upon us by beloved personalities, we eagerly share their gifts as lavishly as we can.

MAKING EXPERIMENTS IN LEADING

Making Merry

Song: "Doing Nothing but Sing."

A person with a light touch leads this bit of relaxation music as an impromptu song for a social gathering.

Pick up the melody from the leader's singing of it. Then add the accompaniment. Exaggerate the dynamics to make it emphatic. Try singing it in slow, medium, and fast movements. Decide which one is most pleasing.

Improvise an orchestra for merriment by cupping the hands and clapping them to sound like a tom-tom. Snap fingers to suggest castanets, shape the hands and sing through them on syllable "who" to imitate a cornet, go through the motions of playing an imaginary violin, etc.—each manipulates an instrument of his imagining. Listen to the surprising effect when all play together keeping time with the piano. Children are not the only ones who know how to imitate!

DOING NOTHING BUT SING

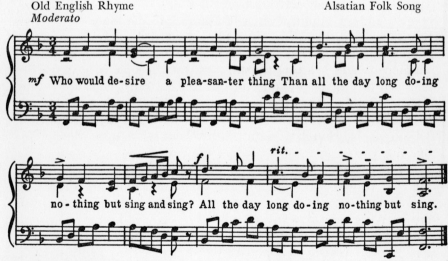

Edith Lovell Thomas, *The Whole World Singing* (The Friendship Press, 1950), p. 13. Used by permission.

136

Singing a Prayer for Guidance

Anthem: "Lead Me, Lord" by Samuel S. Wesley.

Appoint in advance one of the class to conduct the group in singing the anthem for the purpose of inducing the spirit of prayer at the beginning of a service. Secure a guest minister of music from the community to do this if the class cannot provide the leadership desired.

LEAD ME, LORD

Psalms 5:8; 4:8   Samuel S. Wesley

"What Awakes, When Reminded by the Instrument"

Instrumental Selection: "Adagio" by Mendelssohn.

Played by pianist or organist through which the impression of a benediction may be received by the class. Precede with an invitation to accept what the music will give.

ADAGIO

In arpeggio style, pedal throughout   From Felix Mendelssohn, Op. 58

From *Sing, Children Sing,* copyright 1939 by Edith Lovell Thomas, No. 15. Used by permission of Abingdon-Cokesbury Press.

The motivating and response given to each experiment in leading are to be noted and discussed at the finish or following each experiment. What and how the leader did and why will come up for critical comment, appreciation, and suggestion as to better presentations. Try to discover the value, or disvalue, to the group of each musical experience and the causes as you see them.

CHAPTER X

WHEN CELEBRATING

I keep the Eternal at all times before me; with him so close, I cannot fail.

. And so my heart and soul rejoice, my body rests secure; . . .

thou wilt reveal the path to life, to the full joy of thy presence, to the bliss of being close to thee for ever.[1]

Worship is essentially the praise and celebration of life. In worship, man comes before the Lord with psalms and hymns and spiritual songs. As in all celebration, the religious festival is not merely the barren recollection of a good that once was. It is present joy and power, the happiness of an immediate touch of life at its highest and best.[2]

THE great festivals of Christmas and Easter capture the imagination and affection for one reason because of the powerful hold that celebrating an occasion has upon us. Events in the home which turn our thoughts to religion and yield "the happiness of an immediate touch of life at its highest and best"—birthdays, holidays, new jobs, finishing a hard task, travels, even death when seen as entrance into another life—these are fraught with associations full of meaning.

Can we not sound this note of celebration which never fails to call people together on great holy days more frequently in our church and its school? Why not make more of its power felt every time we meet with joy in God's presence?

In her *Ceremonials of Common Days*,[3] Abbie Graham shows how close at hand and ever present are the occasions to be celebrated by joyful hearts. Eyes to see, ears to hear, and eagerness to say and sing

[1] Psalm 16:8, 9, 11 Moffatt.
[2] Von Ogden Vogt, *Modern Worship* (Yale University Press, 1927), p. 12. Used by permission.
[3] Published by the Woman's Press.

our enjoyment of the common and unexpected are enough in-gredients to make a celebration at any time.

One can sense this mood on going into a place made ready for worship in small details, even as in more elaborate ones—the clean-liness, order, better arrangement of furniture, seating, a thing of beauty like a rose, branch of new spring leaves, picture of a singing choir, altar cloth of lovely color, any hint of "something happy on the way." Most convincing of all is the serene, yet expectant spirit of the leader, prepared to give and get from the group something specially fine to match the day and the religious purpose.

Music, an integral element of celebration, largely determines its quality and character; and it has wide enough scope to include all of life. To bring into the sanctuary the talents we have and make glorious the praise of God is of all experiences the most wonderful!

Charles J. Connick, distinguished maker of stained glass, whose radiant rose window glorifies the Cathedral of St. John in New York, traces one of the roots of his love of beauty back to his childhood in a children's day celebration in a country Sunday school:

I see again the shining eyes of the little fellow—myself—his delight in the shimmering fountain (improvised) and its setting of color and sound contrasts distinctly with a droning about dates of wars and deaths of kings in a stuffy and dull sort of place.

Another memory follows . . . years later in a very much larger, uglier, and more sophisticated Sunday school. The youngster was twelve or thirteen, old enough to get an enduring impression of a handsome man . . . superintendent of the Emory Sunday school of Pittsburgh. . . . With a few enthusiastic words he took the psalm we had been studying out of our grubby lesson leaves and made it into a spirited song . . .

> Lift up your heads, O ye gates . . .
> And the King of glory shall come in.[4]

Now I know that on that historic morning he introduced one boy to a golden world of poetry. . . . The Bible was changed as by magic, from a collection of commandments and precepts he was to learn and recite, into an anthology of inspired poems. . . .

I think Wordsworth was right when he said:

> Trailing clouds of glory do we come
> From God who is our home.[5]

[4] Psalm 24 K.J.V.
[5] "Intimations of Immortality."

I feel that Sunday schools are wonderful places to perpetuate the lustre of those clouds of glory.[6]

A junior department, meeting Sundays in a room where the boys and girls took dancing lessons on weekdays, had difficulty in thinking of it as a place of worship. Their superintendent patiently talked and worked with the boys and girls for months on what worship is and how it is expressed. They studied settings devoted to its purposes. Many of the group had never attended a service in a church since their meeting place was a community center. Slowly they came to understand the surroundings and tools which assist the process of worship. Over a long period they labored with teachers making simulated stained-glass windows for the room. One of the fathers made an altar which was placed in front of a large rose window lighted by electricity. The room was so utterly transformed by these symbols in color, the work of their hands, that the spirit of the children changed as they came to use it for its designed purpose.

On a beautiful Sunday in May the new aids to worship were dedicated to celebrate the completion of what had proved to be an arduous and often discouraging task. The essence of the service seemed to reach high expression when the junior choristers, assisted by a soprano soloist from the adult choir, sang Bach's aria, "My heart, ever faithful, sing praises, be joyful, my Jesus is here!" [7]

Some celebrations held in four different churches, contributed to by various age groups and illuminating several areas of high significance, are described here to hint at possibilities that can be variously simplified and adapted.

1. The Bible in Our Church (Order of service abbreviated)

The occasion was the closing service of the church school year at the vesper hour; the purpose, to relate the learnings in the church school to the sanctuary mosaics as they speak to us.

Prelude: "Adoration"	Felix Borowski
"Romance"	Joseph Bonnet
"Idylle"	Harold Greenhill
Processional Hymn: "All Glory, Laud and Honor"	"St. Theodulph"
Opening Sentences: "In the name of the Lord Jesus" (Col. 3:15-17 R.S.V.)	
Congregational Response: "All people that on earth do dwell" (first stanza),	"Old 100th"

[6] *Adventures in Light and Color* (Random House, 1937). Used by permission.
[7] Radburn Community Church, Fair Lawn, New Jersey: Rev. Bedros K. Apelian, Minister.

Sacrament of Baptism:
    (a) Song: "Children, Come!" (Kindergarten, First, Second Grades.) Chinese
    Air.   (Music, Chapter VI)
    (b) Presentation of Children

Dramatic Interpretation: "The Bible in Our Church" by the Church School
    (*a*) Interpreter: Introduction

The church is our religious home. Here we learn to live the joyous life of the Christian family with our Father, God. This beautiful sanctuary is a great picture book of people who share with us their experiences of God. These pictures in colored mosaics we call "The Bible in Our Church." When you understand them, they really speak to you.

High over all is the One for whom our church is named, the Christ, seated as the teacher. His right hand is extended in blessing. His left hand holds the book opened to "I am the light of the world." [8] About him is an ever-glowing light.

Framing the Christ are medallions symbolizing seven gifts of the Spirit, the qualities of true Christians. The unseen verse choir tells their names and explains the signs on their shields.
    (*b*) The Gifts

High-school girls, costumed like the figures that represent seven gifts, carrying shields on which are painted symbols, move into a semicircle before altar.

High-school verse choir, unseen in fourth-floor gallery, and soloist in opposite gallery, present a litany of the gifts antiphonally.

Choir Interlude: "Lovely appear the feet of them that preach and bring good news of peace." (From Oratorio: "The Redemption")   Gounod
    (*c*) Moses with Tablets of the Law (Voice from Old Testament)

One of the men of the church, costumed to reproduce large mosaic figure on right of altar, delivers Moses' message in biblical language.

Choir Chant: "Lord, have mercy upon us and write all these laws in our hearts, we beseech thee"   Tallis
    (*d*) John the Baptist, with staff (Voice from the New Testament)

One of the ministers of the church, costumed to reproduce large mosaic figure on left of altar, delivers John's message in biblical language.

Bass Solo: "But who may abide the day of His coming, and who shall stand when He appeareth?" (From Oratorio: "Messiah")   Handel
    (*e*) The Evangelists (Matthew, Mark, Luke, John—each bears the book
        containing his Gospel and declares his individual word from the Bible)

Young men leaders in the church school represent in costume mosaic figures in half dome of the apse.

Church School Singing and Speaking of Jesus:
Assembled in a large group before the altar singing:
    (*a*) "The Growing Jesus" (Junior Class)   Schubert[9]

---

[8] John 8:12 R.S.V.
[9] Edith Lovell Thomas, *Singing Worship* (Abingdon-Cokesbury Press).

(b) "Jesus Was a Loving Teacher" (Primary Grades)   Barnard[10]
Reading: "He was a real Person, Jesus of Nazareth" Ruth and Mary Hadley[11]
   (High-School Verse Choir)
Choir Hymn of Devotion:

"I bind my heart this tide   "Fealty"[12]
To the Galilean's side."

Act of Remembrance (of the meaning of our church) : The Minister
Prayer
Offertory: "The Swan"   Saint-Saens
Recessional Hymn: "Book of books, our people's strength" "Liebster Jesu"[13]
Benediction
Postlude: "Come, Thou Almighty King," McKinley[14]

This was an exhilarating hour of celebration for the youngest to the oldest of the church family. The glory of religion symbolized in our sanctuary was reflected on the faces of those who sang, spoke, and dramatized the Christian story. To present it adequately months were spent in thoughtful work by the directors of Christian education and music, teachers, ministers, organist, costumer, children, youth, young people, and adults.

The organist selected his numbers to introduce the event on the note of expectancy and to conclude it with the impression of majesty. The melodic offertory with its harplike accompaniment was a kind of light "grace note" played with the children particularly in mind.

The processional struck the keynote of the ceremonial in honor of Jesus with the church's great Palm Sunday hymn and its noble chorale tune:

All glory, laud, and honor,
   To thee, Redeemer, King,
To whom the lips of children
Made sweet hosannas ring.

. . . .

Our praise and prayer and anthems
Before thee we present.[15]

[10] *Hymns for Primary Worship* (Westminster Press) .
[11] Louise B. Griffiths, *Becoming a Person* (Westminster Press, 1942) .
[12] H. Augustine Smith, *The New Hymnal for American Youth* (Fleming H. Revell Co., 1930) .
[13] *The Methodist Hymnal* (1935) .
[14] Christ Church, Methodist, New York, New York: Church School Vesper Service. Mrs. Sam T. Greene, Director of Christian Education; Dr. Ralph W. Sockman, Minister. Used by permission.
[15] St. Theodulph (*ca.* 820) .

A modern hymn about the Bible, set to the stately "Liebster Jesu," German chorale, was the recessional which ended with the prayer:

> Light of Knowledge, ever burning,
> Shed on us thy deathless learning.[16]

The opening sentences from the New Testament, calling upon all the people to "be thankful . . . as you sing Psalms," were answered by the congregation with the paraphrase of the Hundredth Psalm, the Jubilate Deo of Christendom, sung to the Genevan "Old 100th," and beginning:

> All people that on earth do dwell,
> Sing to the Lord with cheerful voice.[17]

Each choice of music for the church school was made with a view to what the particular age group had been learning that it might give to the church family celebration. The Chinese folk air helped the youngest children to get the feeling of other members of God's family beside themselves, in singing how Jesus felt about all children. (Song in Chapter VI.)

A lyrical melody of Schubert's seemed best adapted to junior voices, set to the story of Jesus as a growing boy:

> Along the ways where nature
> Spake low, by hill and glen,
> He grew in wisdom, stature,
> And grace with God and men.[18]

The boys and girls carried on the biography into Jesus' manhood by adding a stanza of their own starting with:

> He grew to be a teacher,
> A helpful, honest friend.

The primary classes continued the tale with a childlike hymn tune, Charlotte A. Barnard's "Brocklesbury," which conveyed a sense of the warm personality of Jesus:

> Jesus was a loving Teacher,
> Helping people day by day.[19]

[16] Percy Dearmer (1925).
[17] William Kethe (1561).
[18] M. W. Stryker.
[19] Wilhelmina D'A. Stephens.

144

In the junior and senior high school groups are boys whose voices are on vacation from singing. A speaking choir is an excellent outlet for this period, in addition to, or with the girls, in place of singing. The reading of the vigorous, graphic sketch "A Real Person," written by two gifted high-school authors, gave those who worked on it for weeks a new conception which they communicated with reality.

The choir completed this sequence on Jesus, built up step by step, with its hymn of personal loyalty to the Galilean Master. They were out of sight behind the choir screen. The singers and readers in front of the altar stood in silence with bowed heads during the singing.

The other choral portions, chant and anthem, furnished musical comments by the trained singers of the Chancel Choir. Thereby they led in prayer with "Lord, have mercy upon us," through the harmonies of Tallis, the sixteenth century English church composer. Our eyes were lifted to bringers of "the good news of peace" down the ages by music from "The Redemption."

The minister conducted the act of remembrance in a few moments of thinking aloud about what the church has given us, taking us into prayer and an offering of gratitude for our heritage.

Judging by remarks heard, "it put us all together," as the junior said of a worship hymn. The dimensions of our oneness were the entire span of life: the height, musical expression from early up to modern worship motifs; the width, Christianity in the local church, a branch of the church universal. The whole was related to the framework of the Bible and the radiance it sheds upon the family of God. Every church building has symbols and associations which its school needs to celebrate in the light of its people's valuation and experience.

2. Youth Choir Service of Good Will

A stranger in a strange city happened into a vesper service on Sunday afternoon, February 12. The church was well filled and an atmosphere of reverence prevailed as the strains of an organ prelude filled the building. Then suddenly from the distance children's voices singing and presently . . . a joyous procession of children and youth, ranging in ages from six or eight years to late teens. A first glance revealed an interesting array of robes: black, black with white surplices, dark blue with light blue surplices, dark red with white surplices, white wool fitted robes with short capes . . . worn by Negro boys and girls . . . national groups in native dress—Russian, Chinese, and Italian. . . . All of the aisles of the church, both upstairs and down, were filled with singing children. They crowded the choir pews, the entire chancel, and both sides of the balcony near the chancel. What was this unusual assemblage—a junior League of Nations or an international convention of childhood? . . . They were singing:

> Lord of all, to thee we raise
> This, our hymn of grateful praise.[20]

This, then, must be but childhood's and youth's joyous expression of praise and worship, without heed to race or religious sect, to a Being whom they recognize as their common Father.

The call to worship was followed by a prayer anthem, sung in Italian by a group of Italian girls. The entire congregation joined in reading the ninety-eighth Psalm. Then a hush lay over the place as the clear sincere voices of teen-age young people sang:

> God, who touchest earth with beauty,
> Make me lovely too.[21]

So the service proceeded. A prayer and the hymn, "Tell Me the Stories of Jesus," sung by a Chinese group, were followed by an antiphonal hymn with scripture reading; then three Negro choirs sang that old Spiritual, "I've Got a Robe," after which a Russian group sang a Russian folk song and a carol. The offertory was Bach's "O Savior Sweet," sung by five choirs. This was followed by "Give Ear Unto Me," sung by boy choristers. There was a congregational hymn and a brief address and then the combined choirs, thirteen in all, arose and sang out a challenge which that adult audience surely cannot soon forget:

> O brother man! fold to thy heart thy brother;
> . . . .
> To worship rightly is to love each other.[22]

Thus ended the "Young People's Choir Service of Good Will" held in Madison Avenue Presbyterian Church, New York City, as a part of the observance of Race Relations Sunday.

The stranger rose and went out into the complexities of a distressed world with renewed hope, having found in the midst of that great city some churches and some leaders and some children and youth who were not afraid to demonstrate their belief that—

> God framed
> Mankind to be one mighty family
> Himself our Father, and the world our home.[23]

This moving picture of Lincoln's birthday celebrated by a host of choirs was taken at the beginning of what has become an annual

---

[20] Folliott S. Pierpoint, "For the beauty of the earth."

[21] Mary S. Edgar.

[22] John Greenleaf Whittier.

[23] This editorial, "That Good Will May Prevail," referring to the First Annual Youth Choir Service of Good Will, was printed in the *International Journal of Religious Education,* April, 1933. Used by permission.

occasion. The root idea as put forth by its originator, Horace M. Hollister, then director of the young people's choirs of the church, was embodied in this quotation printed on the cover of the program:

> In hearts too young for enmity
> There lies the way to make men free.
> When children's friendships are world-wide,
> New ages will be glorified.
> Let child love child, and strife will cease.
> Disarm the hearts, for that is peace.[24]

Mr. Hollister and his wife did all they could to plant the seeds of friendliness among the choristers. By much collaboration with the other directors they took representatives of their choirs to visit and rehearse with every participating choir in the respective churches. These choristers on the day of the service welcomed the guest choristers and made them feel at home because of the earlier contacts.

The service was developed each season to strengthen the spirit of unity by singing more and more items as a combined chorus. Solo and individual choir numbers were avoided to eliminate any temptation to compete in singing worship. Care was exercised in admitting only music and texts that would raise the group from inferior to higher levels of expression. The final anthem has always been Geoffrey Shaw's "Worship" ("O Brother Man"), to underscore the actual practice of interracial co-operation. This tradition appears to take deeper hold on the choirs with each year's repetition.

Celebration of a patriotic holiday with musical worship of this order by a chorus of as many of the world family as can be assembled is a prayer "that good will may prevail" put into action. Any town or country community can conduct a festival of this order to enjoy and perpetuate those aspirations that make our nation great.

3. The Oratorio "Elijah": Mendelssohn

Condensed for choir and congregation.

Jesus took with him Peter and James and John his brother, and led them up a high mountain apart. And he was transfigured before them. . . . And behold, there appeared to them Moses and Elijah, talking with him.[25]

Organ Prelude: Introduction to "Elijah"   Mendelssohn

[24] Ethel Blair Jordan.
[25] Matthew 17:1-3 R.S.V.

Hymn: "God is my strong salvation" Tune: "Aurelia"   Wesley
Invocation
Choral Response: Theme from Chorus, No. 19 (The People)
   "Almighty Father, hear our prayer, and bless all souls that wait before thee."
Responsive Reading

 Minister (Elijah): As God the Lord of Israel liveth before whom I stand, there shall not be dew nor rain these years but according to my word.

 Congregation (Nos. 1 and 2—The People): Help, Lord! Wilt thou quite destroy us? The harvest now is over, the summer days are gone, and yet no power cometh to help us! Will then the Lord be no more God in Zion? The deep affords no water; and the rivers are exhausted! The suckling's tongue now cleaveth for thirst to his mouth; the infant children ask for bread and there is no one to feed them! Lord, bow down thine ear to our prayer!

Tenor Solo (Nos. 3 and 4—Obadiah): Ye people, rend your hearts and not your garments, for your transgressions the prophet Elijah hath sealed the heavens through the word of God. I therefore say to you, forsake your idols, return to God; for he is slow to anger and merciful and kind and gracious and repenteth him of the evil.

  If with all your hearts ye truly seek me ye shall ever surely find me, thus saith our God. Oh! that I knew where I might find him that I might even come before his presence.

Baritone Solo (No. 14—Elijah): Draw near, all ye people. Come to me!

  Lord God of Abraham, Isaac and Israel, this day let it be known that thou art God and I am thy servant! O show to all this people that I have done these things according to thy word! O hear me, Lord, and answer me and show this people that thou art Lord and God and let their hearts again be turned!

Quartet (No. 15—Angels): Cast thy burden upon the Lord and he shall sustain thee. He never will suffer the righteous to fall. He is at thy right hand. Thy mercy, Lord, is great and far above the heavens. Let none be made ashamed that wait upon thee.

Organ Offertory (No. 31—Angel): O Rest in the Lord
Hymn:

'Mid all the traffic of the ways

. . . .

Make in my heart a quiet place.

Tune: "St. Agnes," Dykes

Soprano Solo (No. 21): Hear ye, Israel! Hear what the Lord speaketh: O hadst thou heeded my commandments! Who hath believed our report? To whom is the arm of the Lord revealed? Thus saith the Lord, the Redeemer of Israel, and his Holy One, to him oppressed by tyrants: I am he that comforteth. Be not afraid, for I am thy God. I will strengthen thee. Say, who art thou that thou art afraid of a man that shall die, and forgettest the Lord, thy Maker, who hath stretched forth the heavens and laid the earth's foundations? Be not afraid, for I, thy God, will strengthen thee.

Responsive Reading (No. 25):

Minister (Obadiah): Man of God, now let my words be precious in thy sight. Thus saith Jezebel: "Elijah is worthy to die." So the mighty gather against thee and they have prepared a net for thy steps that they may seize thee, that they may slay thee. Arise, then, and hasten for thy life! To the wilderness journey! The Lord, thy God, doth go with thee. He will not fail thee.

Congregation (No. 26—Elijah): It is enough, O Lord! Now take away my life for I am not better than my fathers. The children of Israel have broken thy covenant, thrown down thine altars and slain all thy prophets with the sword; and I, even I only, am left and they seek my life to take it away.

Women's Chorus (No. 28—Angels): Lift thine eyes to the mountains. Whence cometh help? Thy help cometh from the Lord, Maker of heaven and earth. He hath said thy foot shall not be moved. Thy Keeper will never slumber.

Mixed Chorus (No. 29—Angels): He, watching over Israel, slumbers not nor sleeps. Should'st thou walking in grief, languish, he will quicken thee.

Responsive Reading (No. 31):

Minister (The Angel): O rest in the Lord. Wait patiently for him and he shall give thee thy heart's desires. Commit thy way unto him and trust in him and fret not thyself because of evil doers.

Congregation (No. 33—Elijah): Night falleth round me, O Lord! Be thou not far from me. Hide not thy face from me, O Lord. My soul is thirsting for thee as a thirsty land.

Mixed Chorus (No. 43): And then shall your light break forth as the light of the morning breaketh, and your health shall speedily spring forth then, and the glory of the Lord shall ever reward you. Lord, our Creator, how excellent thy name is in all the nations! Thou fillest heaven with thy glory. Amen.

Hymn: "March on, O soul, with strength"   Tune: "Arthur's Seat," Goss

Benediction

Choral Response: Theme from Chorus, No. 19 (The People)

Hear thou in love, O Lord, our cry,

In heaven, thy dwelling place on high.

Organ Postlude (No. 22): "Be not afraid, saith God, the Lord, thy help is near!" [26]

The Sunday morning service was the time for this act of musical worship, as conceived in Mendelssohn's oratorio, "Elijah." The place of prayer, "oratory," was where the Italian priest Philip Neri in the middle of the sixteenth century conducted popular meetings to interest young people in church attendance through acquainting them with Bible characters. The stories were told, perhaps in

[26] First Methodist Church, South Norwalk, Connecticut. Rev. Charles Wesley Lee, Minister. Used by permission.

costumes, sung and made to live in dramatic style. This new form of interpretation was later called "oratorio" after the building in which it was given.

"Elijah" as shown required congregational participants. Sunday morning was set aside, rather than afternoon or evening, when fuller co-operation could be obtained. The choir had never learned the work before. The soloists were inexperienced, and since the choir was relatively new, getting ready for the unique celebration demanded a great deal of work. The particular season was one that called for courage, vision, and doing something never before attempted. Becoming acquainted with a choral work that large choirs measure up to was a discipline which improved the regular output of the group. The choristers gained a sense of accomplishment which made them feel it was a privilege to offer the results to their church.

The principle of narrating a biblical story in reading, singing, and playing in more or less outline form is one that can be practiced as simply or as elaborately as desired. Recordings of the numbers from sacred oratorios, "Messiah" and other masterpieces, and sufficient background filled in to tell the story are right at hand for lively presentation of music that every child and his elders should know. For illustration of the method well applied, with piano furnishing the themes, consult Angela Diller's arrangement of "Siegfried," the Wagnerian music drama,[27] to see how attractive it can be. Adaptation to sacred works is easily done, and knowledge of great church music can be forwarded thereby.

With all the modern ways of reaching minds through television, radio, and screen we should bestir ourselves to make the cause of religion arresting and seen in more festal dress.

4. Centennial Choral Festival

Processional Hymn: "Rejoice, Ye Pure in Heart" Tune: "Marion," Messiter
Invocation
Call to Worship: "Hebrew Shofar Song" [28] (Baritone solo, Trumpet, and Chorus)

> "And when the Shofar is sounded,
> Hark Ye!"

Anthems:
   "Great and Glorious" (Chancel and Children's Choirs) Clarence Dickinson

---

[27] Published by G. Schirmer.
[28] By Clarence Dickinson. This and all the other anthems are available through H. W. Gray Co., New York, New York.

"Great and glorious is the name of the Lord of Hosts!"
"O God our help in ages past. Amen."

"O Saviour of the World"   G. Palestrina
"O Saviour of the world, who by thy cross and precious blood hast redeemed
us, save us."

"Echo Kyrie" (Children's and Chancel Choirs)   G. Gabrieli

"O Lord God, have mercy."

"Lord, Have Mercy" (Children's and Chancel Choirs)   Serbian Liturgy

"Lord, have mercy upon us"

"O Lord God, Have Mercy" (Men's Voices)   Orlando di Lasso

"Lord, have mercy on me.
O Lord, according to thy great loving kindness, cleanse me now."

"The Pharisee and the Publican"   Heinrich Schuetz
"Holy Angels Singing"   Russian Traditional

(Holy angels singing to shepherds)

"O Saviour Sweet" (Children's and Chancel Choirs)   J. S. Bach

"O Saviour sweet, O Saviour kind"

"Psalm CL"   Cesar Franck
"Alleluia" (Children's Choirs)   Franz Liszt

"Alleluia!
Let all mankind rejoice and sing."

"The Resurrection" (In commemoration of the death of Franz Liszt in 1886)
                                                                Franz Liszt

"Christ is risen."

"Light Celestial"   Peter Tschaikowsky

"Light celestial, supernal glory,
O Jesus Christ, the Son of God."

"For All Who Watch"   Clarence Dickinson

"For all who watch tonight"

Prayer
"Hallelujah Chorus"   G. F. Handel

"Hallelujah! for the
Lord God Omnipotent reigneth."

Benediction
Recessional: "Glorious Things of Thee Are Spoken" Tune: "Austria," Haydn [29]

[29] Celebrating in Riverside Church the founding of Union Theological Seminary,
New York, New York. Used by permission of Clarence Dickinson.

When a small, isolated choir is merged with a chorus of a thousand voices, a component of forty choirs, as in this festival, then does it lose identity to find it on a new and transforming level, never forgotten. The mother of a boy in the children's choir, witnessing it, caught her first glimpse of the real purpose of the weeks of rehearsal. She exclaimed with tears in her eyes, *"This* is what it was for!" A young college man, member of a limited adult choir, remarked breathlessly, "Why, this is . . . is . . . *wonderful!"* At the cafeteria supper, served to the singers between rehearsal and evening program, excitement ran high as the guests mingled, all aglow over the incredulous music they were hearing and making.

The church mediates to her children experiences through such celebrations that seem to be of once-in-a-lifetime importance for those who take part. Can she not use so-called "ordinary" days to "perpetuate the lustre of those clouds of glory" "from God who is our home" in gracious and surprising ways?

Factors which lent significance to this eventful engagement were its comprehensive purpose, the beautiful place where it was held, the number of people in it, and the lofty character and progression of its program. To mark the one-hundredth birthday of an institution which trains and sends out ministers to the churches, its School of Sacred Music, then only eight years old, was asked to celebrate the day with song. The place was the neighboring Riverside Church, large enough to accomodate the throng attending. The beauty and ample facilities of this impressive setting enhanced the service at many points for the choristers and the capacity congregation.

Dr. Clarence Dickinson, director of the school, assembled its students and alumni and instructed them how to rehearse and render the program music. Over forty directors gathered their choirs, one thousand strong, from six states and six denominations to teach them the hymns and anthems. Dr. Dickinson conducted several sectional rehearsals. The one combined chorus sang for the first time under his direction on the afternoon of the day when the festival took place in the evening.

The marvel spoken of by the Old Testament prophet was witnessed "The treasurers of all nations are brought hither and my House here filled with splendour." [30] Never before to our knowledge was there so much rare and inspiring music of the Christian Church brought by the nations to the house of God at one time. Ranging

[30] Haggai 2:7 Moffatt.

from the ancient Hebrew Shofar call to worship on through gifts from Italy, Serbia, Russia, Germany, Austria, France, England, and America. The splendor of the final chorus was almost overwhelming: "He shall reign for ever and ever, King of Kings and Lord of Lords. Hallelujah!" The congregation with the choirs united in the affirmation of the recessional hymn:

> Glorious things of thee are spoken,
> Zion, city of our God.[31]

The choirs dispersed to their homes, awakened to their mission and endued with greater power to serve their own churches because of this choral celebration.

SHALL WE SING FOR JOY TOGETHER?

What finer climax to this course can you conceive than celebrating in singing worship a service prepared by a class committee and conducted by them? Other classes might be invited to participate if the plan is feasible.

Suggestions should be contributed by each member to bring to the fore what is considered most vital. The group might want to lift out of the previous evenings of discussion and sing those numbers illustrated by comments, related experiences, and ideals of greatest reality for the whole company. By aligning these elements in new relationships a fresh sense of their values might be gained and what has emerged that is worth keeping be conserved and vivified. "My house here filled with splendor" could be a motivating idea to draw together the elements which have most "worthship."

In whatever way you conclude be sure that the hour contains expression of something better and more significant than the foregoing periods have brought forth. Aim at putting a climax on what has taken place in the group's progress. Face also new beginnings which each must try in his individual church if he is true to the vision and dream that have come to him during this study-practice.

> Bestir yourself, bestir yourself . . .
> robe yourself with strength! . . .
> Rise, shake the dust from you . . .
> loosen your shackles now.[32]

[31] John Newton.
[32] Isaiah 52:1, 2 Moffatt.

APPENDIX
MUSICAL ILLUSTRATIONS

CHAP.

I. LAUDES DOMINI: "When morning gilds the skies."
   THE FEAST OF LIGHTS (MOOZ ZUR) : "Rock of ages, let our song."

II. LOBET UND PRAISET (round) : "Praise and thanksgiving let everyone bring."
   THE COMPANY OF JESUS: "The simple fishermen."
   AURELIA (with descant) : "The church's one foundation."

III. Improvising: intoning, chanting, harmonizing.
   A HYMN (piano).
   A STORY (piano).
   NUN DANKET: "Now thank we all our God."

IV. DIVINUM MYSTERIUM: "Of the Father's love begotten."
   IN DULCI JUBILO: "In Dulci Jubilo."
   VICTORY: "The strife is o'er, the battle done."
   LIEBSTER JESU: "Blessed Jesus, at thy word."
   THANKSGIVING PSALM: "Come, let us to the Lord shout joyfully."
   PRO PATRIA: "Heralds of Christ, who bear the King's commands."

V. ENGLISH CHRISTMAS CAROL: "The year's at the spring."
   PLUM BLOSSOMS: "Sweet plum blossoms, fine and white."
   SHELTERED DALE: "Awake, awake to love and work."

VI. WHO-EE: " 'Who-ee! Who-ee!' sings the Wind."
   LOOK: "Look! look! our seeds we're planting."
   CHILDREN, COME: "Jesus said long, long ago."

VII. BEFORE WORSHIP: "Walk slowly, be silent."
   LOVING KINDNESS: "The earth is full of the loving kindness of the Lord."
   DOING FRIENDLY THINGS: "When Jesus walked this earth of ours."

VIII. DOING NOTHING BUT SING: "Who would desire a pleasanter thing."
   LEAD ME, LORD: "Lead me, Lord, lead me in thy righteousness."
   ADAGIO (piano).

CAROL AND ANTHEM REFERENCES

Publishers:

D ....Oliver Ditson
G ....H. W. Gray
H ....Charles W. Homeyer
O ....Oxford University Press
ES ....E. C. Schirmer
GS ....G. Schirmer
W ....Westminster Press

Adam-West: "Cantique de Noel" ("O Holy Night") ....G
Austrian Carol—Clarence Dickinson: "Shepherds' Christmas Song" ....G
Bach, J. S.: "Come Together Let Us Sing" ....ES
———: "My Heart Ever Faithful" (from Cantata "God So Loved the World") .....G
Bach-Dickinson: "God, My Shepherd Walks Beside Me" ....G
———: "O Savior Sweet" ....G
Bohemian Carols: "Let Our Gladness Know No End" ....GS
———: "We Bring You Glad Tidings" ....GS
Brahms: "Yea, I Will Comfort You" (from the "Requiem") ....GS

154

Curry, L.: "St. Richard's Prayer" ....W
Dickinson, C.: "A Song in Praise of Heaven and Earth" (Nagler) ....G
——: "Easter Anthem" ....G
——: "For All Who Watch Tonight" ....G
——: "Grace Before Singing" ("God of All Lovely Sounds") ....G
——: "Great and Glorious Is the Lord" ....G
——: Hebrew Shofar Song ....G
——: "List to the Lark" ....G
Dvorak, A.: "God Is My Shepherd" ....GS
Farjeon, H.: "Our Brother Is Born" ....O
Franck, C.: "O Lord, Most Holy" ("Panis Angelicus") ....GS
Gabrieli, G.: "Echo Kyrie" ....G
German Carol—G. Holst: "Christmas Song" ....GS
Gounod, C.: "Lovely Appear Over the Mountains" (from "The Redemption") ...GS
Handel, G. F.: "But Who May Abide the Day of His Coming," and
"Hallelujah" (from "Messiah") ....GS
Hebrew Liturgy: "Adoration" (Antiphon) ....G
Jungst—Seventeenth Century: "While Shepherds Watched Their Flocks" ....G
Kettring, D.: "Come, Let Us Worship God" ....W
Kopolyoff, A.: "Alleluia! Christ Is Risen" ....D
di Lasso: "O Lord God, Have Mercy" ....G
Liszt, F.: "Alleluia! Let All Mankind Rejoice" ....G
——: "The Resurrection" (Christ Is Arisen) ....G
Lockwood, Charlotte: "All Thy Works Praise Thee" ....G
Mendelssohn, F.: Selections from "Elijah" ....GS
Moravian Liturgy—R. Bitgood: "Hosanna" ....G
Ochs, Siegfried (Wrongly attributed to Handel): "Thanks Be to Thee" ....ES
Palestrina: "Adoramus Te" ....G
——: "Come, Let Us Worship" ....H
——: "O Savior of the World" ....G
Praetorius: "Sing We All" ....GS
Praxis-Pietas—K. K. Davis: "Praise to the Lord" ....ES
Roberton, H.: "All in an April Evening" ....GS
——: "Let All the World in Every Corner Sing" ....GS
Russian Traditional: "Holy Angels Singing" ....G
Schuetz, H.: "The Pharisee and the Publican" ....G
Serbian Liturgy: "Lord, Have Mercy" ....G
Shaw, G.: "With a Voice of Singing" ....GS
——: "Worship" ("O Brother Man, Fold to Thy Heart Thy Brother") ....G
Thiman, E.: "A Seasonal Thanksgiving" ....GS
Tschaikowsky, P.: "Light Celestial" ....GS
Welsh—K. K. Davis: "Let All Things Now Living" ....ES
Wesley, S. S.: "Lead Me, Lord" ....G

MUSIC SOURCES

(Tune names in SMALL CAPS)

1. Hymnals:
   B ....Baptist-Disciples, *Christian Worship*, 1941
   C ....Congregational, *Pilgrim Hymnal*, 1935
   E ....Evangelical and Reformed, *Hymnal*, 1941
   L ....United Lutheran, *Common Service Book*, 1918
   M ....Methodist, *Hymnal*, 1939

Mo ....Moravian (United Brethren) , *Hymnal and Liturgies,* 1927
NP ....Northern Presbyterian (U.S.A.) , *Hymnal,* 1937
PE ....Protestant Episcopal, *Hymnal,* 1940
SP ....Southern Presbyterian (U.S.) , *Presbyterian Hymnal,* 1927
Un ....Undenominational, *New Church Hymnal,* 1937

2. Song and Church School Books:

Be ....*Beacon Song and Service Book,* Beacon Press, 1935
HJ ....*Hymns for Junior Worship,* Westminster Press, 1940
HP ....*Hymns for Primary Worship,* Westminster Press, 1946
HY ....*Hymnal for Youth,* Westminster Press, 1951
LU ....*Let Us Be Joyful* (Folk Songs and Play for Juniors) , Co-operative Song
Service, n.d.
M&J ....*Martin and Judy Songs* (Nursery, Kindergarten) , Beacon Press, 1949
NHA .....*The New Hymnal for American Youth,* Fleming H. Revell Company, 1930
O ....*The Oxford Book of Carols,* Oxford University Press, 1939
RN ....*Religious Nurture in Nursery Class and Home,* Graded Press, 1942
SC ....*Sing, Children Sing* (Primary) , Abingdon-Cokesbury Press, 1939
SW .*Singing Worship with Boys and Girls* (Junior) , Abingdon-Cokesbury Press, 1935
WW ....*The Whole World Singing* (Junior and older) , Friendship Press, 1950
* ....Included in this text

"A mighty fortress," EIN' FESTE BURG: (1) B, C, E, L, M, Mo, NP, PE, SP, Un; (2) Be, HY, NHA
A ROUND OF THANKS (grace) , "For health and strength": (2) LU
AGNI, "Temper my spirit, O Lord": (2) HY, NHA
"All creatures of our God," LASST UNS ERFREUEN: (1) B, E, M, Un; (2) Be, HJ, HP, HY, LU, NHA, SW
"All glory, laud, and honor," ST. THEODULPH: (1) B, C, E, L, M, Mo, NP, PE, SP, Un; (2) HJ, HP, HY, NHA, SW, WW
"All people that on earth do dwell," OLD 100TH: (1) C, E, M, Mo, NP, PE, Un; (2) Be, HJ, HP, HY, SW, WW
ALL THE WORLD, "Let all the world in every corner sing": (1) M; (2) HJ, HY, WW
"All things bright and beautiful," ROYAL OAK: (1) M, PE; (2) SC
ANTIOCH, "Joy to the world"; (1) B, C, E, L, M, Mo, NP, SP, Un; (2) HY, NHA, SW
ARTHUR'S SEAT, "March on, O soul, with strength": (1) B, C, E, M, NP, SP, Un; (2) HY, NHA
AURELIA, "The church's one foundation": (1) B, C, E, L, M, Mo, NP, PE, SP, Un; (2) HY, NHA, *p. 34
AUSTRIA, "Glorious things of thee are spoken": (1) B, C, E, L, M, Mo, NP, PE, SP, Un; (2) HY
"Awake, awake to love and work," SHELTERED DALE: (1) B, M, Un; (2) *p. 77
BEFORE WORSHIP, "Walk slowly, be silent": (2) WW, *p. 103
BERTHOLD, "With happy voices ringing": (1) B, E, NP, Un; (2) HJ, NHA, SW
"Blessed Jesus," LIEBSTER JESU: (1) E, L, M, Mo, PE, Un; (2) SW, *p. 64
BROCKLESBURY, "Jesus was a loving teacher": (2) HP
CHILDREN, COME, "Jesus said long, long ago": (2) *p. 94
"Christ the Lord [Jesus Christ] is risen today," EASTER HYMN: (1) B, C, E, L, M, Mo, SP, Un; (2) HJ, HP, HY, NHA, SW
CHRISTMAS SONG, "There's a song in the air": (1) B, C, M, Un; (2) HJ, HY, NHA, SW
CHRISTUS, DER IST MEIN LEBEN, "Thank thee, God": (2) WW
"Come, let us to the Lord shout joyfully," THANKSGIVING PSALM: (2) *p. 65
"Come, my soul, thou must be waking," HAYDN: (1) B, C, E, L, M, Un

"Come, ye thankful people," ST. GEORGE'S, WINDSOR: (1) B, C, E, L, M, Mo, NP, PE, Un; (2) Be, HJ, HP, HY, NHA, SW

CRUSADER'S HYMN, "Fairest Lord Jesus": (1) B, C, E, M, Mo, NP, PE, SP, Un; (2) HJ, HY, NHA, SC, SW

CWM RHONDDA, "God of grace and God of glory": (1) M; (2) HY

DECISION, "To every man there openeth": (2) NHA

DIVINUM MYSTERIUM, "Of the Father's love begotten": (1) E, L, PE; (2) HY, *p. 61

DIX, "For the beauty of the earth" (refrain: "Lord of all, to thee we raise") : (1) B, C, E, M, NP, SP, Un; (2) Be, HJ, HY, LU, NHA, SW

DOING FRIENDLY THINGS, "When Jesus walked this earth": (2) SC, *p. 106

DOING NOTHING BUT SING, "Who would desire a pleasanter thing": (2) WW, *p. 136

DRESE, "Not Jerusalem; rather Bethlehem" (second stanza of "Jesus, call thou me") : (1) Mo

EASTER HYMN, "Christ the Lord [Jesus Christ] is risen today": (1) B, C, E, L, M, Mo, SP, Un; (2) HJ, HP, HY, NHA, SW

EIN' FESTE BURG, "A mighty fortress": (1) B, C, E, L, M, Mo, NP, PE, SP, Un; (2) Be, HY, NHA

"Every morning seems to say," SOMETHING HAPPY: (2) M&J

"Fairest Lord Jesus," CRUSADER'S HYMN: (1) B, C, E, M, Mo, NP, PE, SP, Un; (2) HJ, HY, NHA, SC, SW

FAITHFUL, "O joyous Easter morning": (2) NHA

"Far away in old Judea," JUDEA: (2) SW, WW

"Father in heaven, who lovest all," LLEDROD: (1) PE

FEALTY, "I bind my heart this tide": (1) B; (2) HY, NHA

"For all the saints who from their labors rest," SINE NOMINE: (1) B, C, E, M, NP, PE, Un; (2) Be, HY, NHA

"For health and strength" (grace) , A ROUND THANKS: (2) LU

"For the beauty of the earth" (refrain: "Lord of all, to thee we raise") , DIX: (1) B, C, E, M, NP, SP, Un; (2) Be, HJ, HY, LU, NHA, SW

"Give food to all," TABLE GRACE: (2) SC

"Gladly to the house of worship come we," HOUSE OF WORSHIP: (2) SW

GLEN BERNARD, "God, who touchest earth with beauty": (2) SW

"Glorious things of thee are spoken," AUSTRIA: (1) B, C, E, L, M, Mo, NP, PE, SP, Un; (2) HY

"God of grace and God of glory," CWM RHONDDA: (1) M; (2) HY

"God of the prophets," TOULON (OLD 124TH) : (1) B, C, E, Mo, PE, Un

"God, who touchest earth with beauty," GLEN BERNARD: (2) SW

"Good Christian men, rejoice," "In dulci jubilo," IN DULCI JUBILO: (1) B, C, E, M, NP, PE, Un; (2) Be, HY, O, SW, *p. 62

"Good King Wenceslas," GOOD KING WENCESLAS: (2) O

HAMBURG, "When I survey the wondrous cross": (1) B, C, E, NP, SP, Un; (2) HY, NHA

HANOVER, "Ye servants of God, your Master proclaim": (1) B, C, M

HAPPY NEW YEAR, "The little new year is coming in": (2) *p. 87.

HAYDN, "Come, my soul, thou must be waking": (1) B, C, E, L, M, Un

"He who would valiant be," ST. DUNSTAN'S: (1) B, C, E, NP, PE, Un; (2) HY, NHA

"Heralds of Christ," PRO PATRIA: (2) NHA, *p. 66

"Holy, holy, holy is the Lord of hosts" (response) , SANCTUS: (1) B; (2) HY, NHA

HOSANNA, "Thy palm trees fed with dew and sun": (2) NHA

HOUSES OF WORSHIP, "Gladly to the house of worship come we": (2) SW

HYMN TO JOY, "Joyful, joyful, we adore thee": (1) B, E, L, M, NP, SP, Un; (2) Be, HJ, HY, NHA

"I bind my heart this tide," FEALTY: (1) B; (2) HY, NHA

"I'll praise my Maker," OLD 113TH (LUCERNE) : (1) M

"In Christ there is no East or West," ST. PETER: (1) B, C, E, M, NP, SP, Un; (2) HJ, HY, NHA, SW

IN CORDE MEO (response), "Let [May] the words of my mouth": (1) C, SP, Un; (2) NHA

IN DULCI JUBILO, "In dulci jubilo," "Good Christian men, rejoice": (1) B, C, E, M, NP, PE, Un; (2) Be, HY, O, SW, *p. 62

"Into the woods my Master went," LANIER: (1) B, M, SP, Un; (2) HY, NHA

"Jesus said long, long ago," CHILDREN, COME: (2) *p. 94

"Jesus was a loving teacher," BROCKLESBURY: (2) HP

"Joy to the world," ANTIOCH: (1) B, C, E, L, M, Mo, NP, SP, Un; (2) HY, NHA, SW

"Joyful, joyful, we adore thee," HYMN TO JOY: (1) B, E, L, M, NP, SP, Un; (2) Be, HJ, HY, NHA

JUDEA, "Far away in old Judea": (2) SW, WW

KINGS OF ORIENT, "We three kings of Orient are": (1) B, C, M, PE; (2) Be, HY, NHA, O, SW

KREMSER (NETHERLANDS FOLK SONG), "We gather together": (1) B, C, E, M, NP, PE, Un; (2) Be, NHA

LANHERNE, "O brother man, fold to thy heart thy brother": (1) C

LANIER, "Into the woods my Master went": (1) B, M, SP, Un; (2) HY, NHA

LASST UNS ERFREUEN, "All creatures of our God": (1) B, E, M, Un; (2) Be, HJ, HP, HY, LU, NHA, SW

LAUDES DOMINI, "When morning gilds the skies": (1) B, C, E, L, M, Mo, NP, PE, SP, Un; (2) HJ, HY, NHA, SW, *p. 18

LEONI, "The God of Abraham praise": (1) C, E, L, M, NP, PE, Un; (2) HJ, HY

"Let all the world in every corner sing," ALL THE WORLD: (1) M; (2) HJ, HY, WW. UNIVERSAL PRAISE: (1) PE, Un

"Let [May] the words of my mouth," IN CORDE MEO (response): (1) C, SP, Un; (2) NHA

LIEBSTER JESU, "Book of books": (1) E, L, M, Mo, PE, Un; (2) SW, *p. 64

LLEDROD, "Father in heaven, who lovest all": (1) PE

LOBE DEN HERREN, "Praise to the Lord, the Almighty": (1) B, C, L, M, PE, Un; (2) Be, HY, NHA, SW

LOBET UND PRAISET (round), "Praise and thanksgiving": (2) WW, *p. 31

LOOK, "Look! look! our seeds we're planting": (2) M&J, *p. 93

"Lord, have mercy" (chant): (1) M

"Lord, I want to be a Christian," SPIRITUAL: (2) HJ, HP, HY, LU

"Lord of all, to thee we raise" (refrain: "For the beauty of the earth"), DIX: (1) B, C, E, M, NP, SP, Un; (2) Be, HJ, HY, LU, NHA, SW

LOVING KINDNESS, "The earth is full of the loving kindness": (2) SC, *p. 104

LUCERNE (OLD 113TH), "I'll praise my Maker": (1) M

"March on, O soul, with strength," ARTHUR'S SEAT: (1) B, C, E, M, NP, SP, Un; (2) HY, NHA

MARION, "Rejoice, ye pure in heart": (1) B, C, E, L, M, NP, PE, Un; (2) Be, HY, NHA, SW

MEIRIONYDD: (1) B, E, M

" 'Mid all the traffic of the ways," ST. AGNES: (1) E, M, NP, SP, Un; (2) HY, NHA

MOOZ ZUR (THE FEAST OF LIGHTS), "Rock of ages, let our song": (2) HJ, SW, *p. 20

"Morning [noontime, evening] is here," PRAISE FOR BREAD (grace): (2) LU

NETHERLANDS FOLK SONG (KREMSER), "We gather together": (1) B, C, E, M, NP, PE, Un; (2) Be, NHA

"Not Jerusalem; rather Bethlehem" (second stanza of "Jesus, call thou me"), DRESE: (1) Mo

"Now thank we all our God," NUN DANKET: (1) B, C, E, L, M, Mo, PE, SP, Un; (2) Be, HJ, HY, NHA, SC, SW, *p. 47

NUN DANKET, "Now thank we all our God": (1) B, C, E, L, M, Mo, PE, SP, Un; (2) Be, HJ, HY, NHA, SC, SW, *p. 47

"O brother man, fold to thy heart thy brother," LANHERNE: (1) C

"O come, let us sing," VENITE (chant): (1) M, NP, Un

"O God, our help," ST. ANNE: (1) B, C, E, L, M, Mo, NP, PE, SP, Un; (2) Be, HJ, HY, NHA, SW

"O joyous Easter morning," FAITHFUL: (2) NHA

"O Lord of life, thy quickening voice," SOHO: (2) NHA

"O praise ye the Lord," PSALM 150: (2) SW, WW

"Of the Father's love begotten," DIVINUM MYSTERIUM: (1) E, L, PE: (2) HY, *p. 61

OLD 100TH, "All people that on earth do dwell": (1) C, E, M, Mo, NP, PE, Un; (2) Be, HJ, HP, HY, SW, WW

OLD 113TH (LUCERNE), "I'll praise my Maker": (1) M

OLD 124TH (TOULON), "God of the prophets": (1) B, C, E, Mo, PE, Un

"Our Father, who art in heaven," THE LORD'S PRAYER (CHANT): (1) B, C, E, SP, Un; (2) HJ, HY

PIPPA'S SONG, "The year's at the spring": (2) SW, *p. 69

PLUM BLOSSOMS, "Sweet plum blossoms": (2) M&J, SC, *p. 76

"Praise and thanksgiving" (round), LOBET UND PRAISET: (2) WW, *p. 31

PRAISE FOR BREAD, "Morning [noontime, evening] is here": (2) LU

"Praise to the Lord, the Almighty," LOBE DEN HERREN: (1) B, C, L, M, PE, Un; (2) Be, HY, NHA, SW

PRO PATRIA, "Heralds of Christ": (2) NHA, *p. 66

PSALM 150, "O praise ye the Lord": (2) SW, WW

"Rejoice, ye pure in heart," MARION: (1) B, C, E, L, M, NP, PE, Un; (2) Be, HY, NHA

"Rock of ages, let our song," THE FEAST OF LIGHTS (MOOZ ZUR): (2) HJ, SW, *p. 20

ROYAL OAK, "All things bright and beautiful": (1) M, PE; (2) SC

ST. AGNES, " 'Mid all the traffic of the ways": (1) E, M, NP, SP, Un; (2) HY, NHA

ST. ANNE, "O God, our help": (1) B, C, E, L, M, Mo, NP, PE, SP, Un; (2) Be, HJ, HY, NHA, SW

ST. COLUMBA, "The King of love my Shepherd is": (1) PE; (2) Be

ST. DUNSTAN'S, "He who would valiant be": (1) B, C, E, NP, PE, Un; (2) HY, NHA

ST. GEORGE'S, WINDSOR, "Come, ye thankful people": (1) B, C, E, L, M, Mo, NP, PE, Un; (2) Be, HJ, HP, HY, NHA, SW

ST. PETER, "In Christ there is no East or West": (1) B, C, E, M, NP, SP, Un; (2) HJ, HY, NHA, SW

ST. THEODULPH, "All glory, laud, and honor": (1) B, C, E, L, M, Mo, NP, PE, SP, Un; (2) HJ, HP, HY, NHA, SW, WW

SANCTUS (response), "Holy, holy, holy is the Lord of hosts": (1) B; (2) HY, NHA

SHELTERED DALE, "Awake, awake to love and work": (1) B, M, Un; (2) *p. 77

"Silent Night," STILLE NACHT: (1) B, C, E, L, M, Mo, NP, PE, SP, Un; (2) Be, HJ, HP, HY, NHA, SC, SW

SINE NOMINE, "For all the saints who from their labors rest": (1) B, C, E, M, NP, PE, Un; (2) Be, HY, NHA

SOHO, "O Lord of life, thy quickening voice": (2) NHA

SOMETHING HAPPY, "Every morning seems to say": (2) M&J

SPIRITUAL, "Lord, I want to be a Christian": (2) HJ, HP, HY, LU

STILLE NACHT, "Silent night": (1) B, C, E, L, M, Mo, NP, PE, SP, Un; (2) Be, HJ, HP, HY, NHA, SC, SW

STORIES OF JESUS, "Tell me the stories of Jesus": (1) B, M; (2) HJ, HP, SC, WW

"Sweet plum blossoms," PLUM BLOSSOMS: (2) M&J, SC, *p. 76

TABLE GRACE, "Give food to all": (2) SC

"Tell me the stories of Jesus," STORIES OF JESUS: (1) B, M; (2) HJ, HP, SC, WW

"Temper my spirit, O Lord," AGNI: (2) HY, NHA

TERRA BEATA, "This is my Father's world": (1) B, C, E, M, NP, Un: (2) Be, HJ, HY, LU, NHA, SW, WW

"Thank thee, God," CHRISTUS, DER IST MEIN LEBEN: (2) WW

THANK YOU, GOD, "When I'm very happy": (2) RN, *p. 89

THANKSGIVING PSALM, "Come, let us to the Lord shout joyfully": (2) *p. 65

"The church's one foundation," AURELIA: (1) B, C, E, L, M, Mo, NP, PE, SP, Un; (2) HY, NHA, *p. 34

THE COMPANY OF JESUS, "The simple fishermen cast nets": (2) WW, *p. 32

"The earth is full of the loving kindness," LOVING KINDNESS: (2) SC, *p. 104

THE FEAST OF LIGHTS (MOOZ ZUR), "Rock of ages, let our song": (2) HJ, SW, *p. 20

THE FIRST NOWELL, "The first Nowell": (1) B, C, E, M, PE, Un; (2) Be, HJ, HY, NHA

THE GLAD TIME, "When each one has a secret": (2) SC

"The God of Abraham praise," LEONI: (1) C, E, L, M, NP, PE, Un; (2) HJ, HY

THE GROWING JESUS, "The helper of his mother": (2) SW

"The helper of his mother," THE GROWING JESUS: (2) SW

"The King of love my Shepherd is," ST. COLUMBA: (1) PE; (2) Be

"The little new year is coming in," HAPPY NEW YEAR: (2) *p. 87

THE LORD'S PRAYER (chant), "Our Father, who art in heaven": (1) B, C, E, SP, Un; (2) HJ, HY

"The simple fishermen cast nets," THE COMPANY OF JESUS: (2) WW, *p. 32

"The strife is o'er," VICTORY: (1) B, M, NP, PE, Un; (2) HY, NHA, *p. 63

"The year's at the spring," PIPPA'S SONG: (2) SW, *p. 69

"There's a song in the air," CHRISTMAS: (1) B, C, M, Un; (2) HJ, HY, NHA, SW

"This is my Father's world," TERRA BEATA: (1) B, C, E, M, NP, Un; (2) Be, HJ, HY, LU, NHA, SW, WW

"Thy palm trees fed with dew and sun," HOSANNA: (2) NHA

"To every man there openeth," DECISION: (2) NHA

TOULON (OLD 124TH), "God of the prophets": (1) B, C, E, Mo, PE, Un

UNIVERSAL PRAISE, "Let all the world in every corner sing": (1) PE, Un

VENI EMMANUEL, "O come, O come, Emmanuel": (1) B, M, NP, PE, Un; (2) Be, HP, HJ, HY, NHA

VENITE (chant), "O come, let us sing": (1) M, NP, Un

VICTORY, "The strife is o'er": (1) B, M, NP, PE, Un; (2) HY, NHA, *p. 63

"Walk slowly," BEFORE WORSHIP: (2) WW, *p. 103

"We gather together," NETHERLANDS FOLK SONG (KREMSER): (1) B, C, E, M, NP, PE, Un; (2) Be, NHA

"We three kings of Orient are," KINGS OF ORIENT: (1) B, C, M, PE; (2) Be, HY, NHA, O, SW

"When each one has a secret," THE GLAD TIME: (2) SC

"When I survey the wondrous cross," HAMBURG: (1) B, C, E, NP, SP, Un; (2) HY, NHA

"When I'm very happy," THANK YOU, GOD: (2) RN, *p. 89

"When Jesus walked this earth," DOING FRIENDLY THINGS: (2) SC, *p. 106

"When morning gilds the skies," LAUDES DOMINI: (1) B, C, E, L, M, Mo, NP, PE, SP, Un; (2) HJ, HY, NHA, SW

"While shepherds watched their flocks," WINCHESTER OLD: (1) C, PE

"Who would desire a pleasanter thing," DOING NOTHING BUT SING: (2) WW, *p. 136

WHO-EE, " 'Who-ee! who-ee!' sings the Wind": (2) M&J, *p. 91

WINCHESTER OLD, "While shepherds watched their flocks": (1) C, PE

"With happy voices ringing," BERTHOLD: (1) B, E, NP, Un; (2) HJ, NHA, SW

"Ye servants of God, your Master proclaim," HANOVER: (1) B, C, M